Action for Children

Action for Children

Towards an Optimum Child Care Package in Africa

Ideas and proposals based on the proceedings of the Dag Hammarskjöld Seminar on the Dilemma of Quality, Quantity and Cost in African Child Care, organized by the Ethio-Swedish Paediatric Clinic and the Dag Hammarskjöld Foundation in cooperation with the United Nations Economic Commission for Africa, Addis Ababa, 14 to 19 May 1973

Edited by Olle Nordberg, Peter Phillips and Göran Sterky
With a Foreword by T. Peter Omari

THE DAG HAMMARSKJÖLD FOUNDATION,
UPPSALA, 1975

General editor: Sven Hamrell

*The 1973 Dag Hammarskjöld Seminar on the Dilemma of
Quality, Quantity and Cost in African Child Care was financed
by a grant from the Swedish International Development
Authority.*

Layout: Peter Phillips and Thomas Borgström

Set in IBM Composer and printed in Sweden by Borgströms
Tryckeri AB, Motala

Contents

Foreword

Children and women have traditionally been low as priority considerations in African society. Modern enlightenment has not yet made any significant dent in this thinking, and they continue to rank low in the social, economic and political priorities. Lacking spokesmen and leverage, it is little wonder that their plight has continued unabated and unheralded. If traditional African society were to be likened to a boat filled with men, women and children; and if the boat were sinking, I can well entertain the vision of men leaving first, followed next by the women and finally by the children. Value systems are different in Africa and it will obviously require a massive re-education and concerted effort on the part of all concerned in any attempt at re-ordering the rank of priorities in favour of children and women. Fortunately African women can form a powerful political and economic group once awakened to potentialities. Any effort in this direction is to the benefit of the community as a whole.

I am reminded of the time in 1958 when the first and only qualified paediatrician returned to his home country in Ghana from the USA proud of the fact that he could devote his newly acquired knowledge to saving the lives of children and promoting their good health. To his disappointment, and to that of all of us, he was informed that there was no post of paediatrician in the medical service of the country to which he could be appointed and, further, that paediatricians were not needed. There were, of course, specialists of all shades in the country but a doctor for children was not needed or wanted.

As a favour to him for being foolish enough to specialize in a subject or field for which there was no market, he was offered a post in an outlying hospital as a 'general practitioner'. I remember that we all supported his refusal to work as a GP until his qualifications and concern were recognized. Fortunately the Army Medical Service was persuaded to establish a post of paediatrician at the military hospital in Accra and he was promptly appointed to it. Now there are a few more paediatricians in the country.

This incident occurred in 1958 but the situation has not changed much in the rest of Africa. Mothers continue to deliver without the benefit of any medical treatment, anaesthetics or postnatal care. Babies are born without benefit of prenatal and postnatal care; and they continue to die in great numbers as if it were the will of God.

In Ethiopia, the rainy season does not pass without havoc being wreaked upon innocent lives because of lack of proper housing, warmth and medical care. Other countries in Africa contribute to their share of this 'massacre of the innocents', as though the responsibility of governments and parents stopped with assessment of taxes and tax evasion respectively. Religion and politics have often conspired against the child in the less-developed countries, for the children have had no spokesman.

The situation does not demand any exaggeration to convey the plight of mothers and children in Africa. Fathers, who can become politicians or business men and rise to hold positions of influence and who can therefore do something about this situation, are not always aware of what is going on outside their own family or class circles. Very often, because they have no problem of starvation and malnutrition and can afford modern treatment in the best hospitals for themselves and their children, they assume that all is well in the land. Mothers - especially rural mothers - who must bear the brunt of delivering dead babies, looking after helpless children and keeping vigil over incurably sick babies but having no political or economic power to make their voices heard, are condemned to a life of harassment and pain, amid continuous misery and suffering.

We admit shortage of finance, human and physical resources in any programme to combat the scourge of children and to promote their welfare. I am persuaded to think that the will and inclination are lacking even more, even if, in the effort to save lives - be it of children or of adults - we naturally must think of resources and facilities and thus in economic terms.

Amidst all these problems there are men and women, governments and individuals, who have sought to provide direction and support for programmes and institutions. Unicef was the first major instrument for the recognition of the plight of children throughout the less-developed world. The global approach must, however, be supported by organized local - especially governmental - effort. The Ethio-Swedish Paediatric Clinic represents one such practical effort which, over the years, has combined international support with government assistance and the dedicated effort of local and international staff who, through research, educational means and treatment, have sought to combat maternal death with supervised deliveries; infant mortality with perinatal care; malnutrition with development of easily digestible infant dietary preparations from local resources at prices within the range of mothers; and better child care and child health with visual aids and health-education programmes. It is left for the lessons that have been learned to be more widely propagated.

The 1973 Ethio-Swedish Paediatric Clinic/Economic Commission for Africa/ Dag Hammarskjöld Foundation Seminar, the results of which are presented here, has been the labour of love of those who conceived the idea and executed it, as well as of those who have edited and given us this publication. We do not yet have all the answers to better child care in Africa here. The idea of the 'optimum package' presented here needs to be subjected to further examination. But it is clear that this concept and this seminar have broken new ground.

'Optimum package' should not become one of the new jargon terms that plague us from time to time. It describes a programme that can be applied to actual situations. Recognition of the social basis of medical and health practice is one of the major achievements of the seminar, which brought together not only doctors - medical specialists and administrators - nurses and public-health workers but also, what is most important, sociologists, social workers and educationists, and the concept of the optimum package. There should be no rigid boundaries between sociology and medical science in developing Africa. Cooperation should be cultivated and fostered. In fact, the social basis of life in Africa is so strong and so all-pervading that neither health, industry, commerce nor politics can succeed without a proper understanding of the society and its culture. By the social basis is meant also the place of religion in the life of the people.

I hope that the results of the 1973 seminar presented here will serve to spur further research and further action. I would, however, hope that this will not be the only publication to come out of the work of the Ethio-Swedish Paediatric Clinic and its cooperation with the Swedish International Development Authority. Many of the participants and contributors have indicated lines and areas for further development. The immediate priority is for an action programme, even on a limited scale, that would demonstrate in practice, and preferably in the rural setting, the benefits to be derived from the implementation of the optimum package. A possible by-product of this would be the expansion of the Ethio-Swedish Paediatric Clinic into (or the establishment in Africa of) a Pan-African centre for the study of the child where medical specialists, psychologists, sociologists, social workers and educationists would work together to find cures for children's diseases, carry out research into patterns of child growth and behaviour, and devise communications and mass-media facilities and techniques to disseminate information intended to promote the adoption of improved child-care methods.

But it is left for all of us to continue to find further avenues for persuading governments, voluntary and national organizations, institutions and individuals to take seriously the plight of children in Africa so that something may be done about it; and to offer them direction so that wasted effort may be spared in the undertaking.

Addis Ababa,
2 April 1975

T. Peter Omari

Chief,
Social Development Section,
United Nations Economic
Commission for Africa

Introduction

There is no wealth but Life.
John Ruskin, *Unto This Last*

Three decades of international endeavour in the effort to create a world order
founded upon peace and justice have had only a limited success. Humanity is at a
new crisis point, haunted by an awareness of the global problem. Time pressure has
added a stark dimension of grimness to the difficulties that confront mankind:
hunger, sickness, homelessness and cultural deprivation, compounded by the spectre
of an uncontrolled population explosion whose sheer magnitude will take human
history - the whole adventure of man - into a phase that is unlike any that ever
existed before.

Time is not on our side The time pressure is made yet more dramatic by the growing realization that there
is a limit to the world's resources and by the awareness that outmoded *laissez-faire*
mechanisms are no longer adequate in the management of world affairs. For the
unlimited territorial and resource frontiers of old-fashioned nineteenth-century

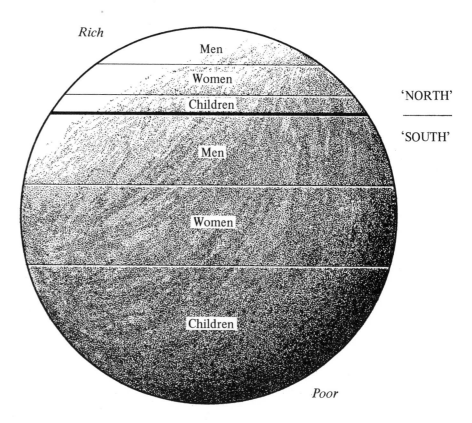

The rich and the poor (the survivors)

imperialism have been replaced by the world of closed systems - the world is in a phase of techno-social coalescence without, as yet, a corresponding consciousness of the need to accept that a historic turning-point has been reached, that we are now also at a psychological frontier.

There are signs in the international forum that efforts are being made to transcend the grave difficulties that confront us: the Cocoyoc Declaration of October 1974 by thirty-two ministers, heads of UN agencies, and social and natural scientists on the need for major changes to meet the basic needs of the world's poorest peoples, and the Dag Hammarskjöld Project on Development and International Co-operation for presentation to the September 1975 Special Session of the General Assembly of the United Nations on a new economic order represent initiatives that are intended to combat the pervasive pessimism generated by the present disorder in world affairs.

In this context the plight of the child has a key significance. The increasing efficiency, in commercial and technological terms, of conventional curative medicine masks the inhumanity of infant neglect and child mortality. We must ask ourselves whether much of the Third World - or 'the South' in contrast to the industrialized countries in 'the North' - is to become a vast sickness pool of starving children deprived of life in its richest sense and menaced by the threat of premature death; and this question may be particularly relevant in the case of Africa with very little health care available to the rural poor, whose true problem and solution lie in the continent's need for economic independence and self-reliance.

The example of China The example of the People's Republic of China is instructive. National statistics are not available on the state of health of China's population - the Chinese approach is that help is more important than statistics - but 'recent visitors report a nation of healthy-looking, vigorous people. Although much of China is still poorly developed technologically and its people - particularly in the rural areas - work very hard for long hours, there is no evidence of the malnutrition, infectious disease or other manifestations of ill health that often accompany this level of development' (WHO/Unicef, 1975). Nowhere in the world has such a poor country made such giant strides in this and in other fields, and for such an enormous population. Improvements in the level of health are not the result of health care alone: nutrition, sanitation and shelter are important. Food is available at prices that are well below those in most developing countries; prevention receives priority in health services as well as in medical education; auxiliary health personnel are at work on the ground, in the rural community where the mass problem is most pressing.

The Chinese model is perhaps not so easy to transfer to other Third World countries, especially those which had only native medicine in the past. It must be remembered, for example, that Chinese medicine was not backward or merely embryonic before the introduction of western technology. Chinese traditional medicine had already reached a considerable level of sophistication, in the use of medicines as well as of techniques, a Chinese medical corps already existed and the traditional input still continues within the total service. It may be, however, that objections to the Chinese example spring largely from western apprehensions based on Eurocentric social values. It could be argued that the traditional African background is in fact highly appropriate for a transfer of the Chinese model and the native practitioners could well be absorbed into the programme, with much advantage.

A major difference between the Chinese model and the western is in the extent to which the former relies for its effectiveness upon the encouragement of popular self-reliance and self-help in the promotion of the health programme. Great efforts have been made to destroy fatalistic attitudes and to promote the idea of mass participation and learning through doing. The Chinese medical profession has itself been obliged to undergo a drastic reorientation, especially from about 1965 onwards, and periods of service in the rural areas are required of most specialists. It is intended that the push for progress should come from the people themselves. In the western model, in so far as it is emulated in Africa, the approach is still based upon the stratification and separation of programmes and staff, vertically rather than horizontally, with the town-bound medical elites administering the 'hand-out' health idea. The very vocabulary reflects the values of this system. 'Professional' staff, so-called, are by definition those who have specialist knowledge or longer training, while the remainder, even if they spend their lives working in the health service, are by implication 'unprofessional'. Most of the western writers on health staffing structures still talk in terms of 'pyramids', at whose apex is the solitary 'professional', literally superior to the mass below. No transfer of the Chinese model is possible to intellectual climates where such notions are still predominant.

Fewer doctors means more auxiliaries for the same price

Certainly, the use of auxiliary health personnel (barefoot doctors) has many implications, not least in its social repercussions. The western-type medicine of many poor areas of the world (Latin America, for example) continues in many ways to embody the authoritarian model bequeathed to it from the nineteenth century, with the patient, where any service is available, as the passive, atomized social unit, waiting endlessly for disposal in the doctor's antechamber. The simple fact of replacing one old-style physician by anything from twenty to forty auxiliaries for the same price may at one and the same time produce greater cost-effectiveness (where trained personnel of any level are in short supply), reduce to a certain extent the high rate of rural unemployment, improve the diminished image of the health service and, possibly, contribute to the reduction of corruption in medicine by the greater universalization of health care. A brain-drain of medical auxiliaries planning to complete their medical degrees in, for example, the USA would imply a much more equitable sharing of medical education costs than is at present the case. (It has been estimated that the annual loss to Latin America due to the flow of physicians to the United States is equal to the total medical aid given by the latter to Latin

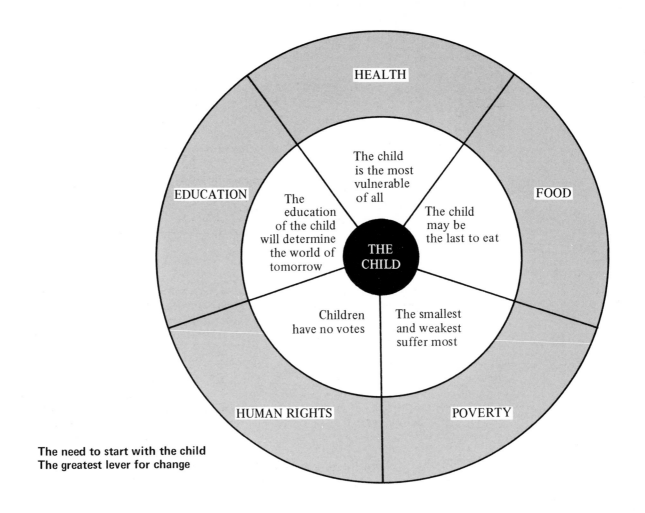

The need to start with the child
The greatest lever for change

America during the decade of the 1960s.) Greater emphasis on auxiliaries might also help in correcting the present gross imbalance in favour of curative medicine to the detriment of prevention. China is not the only country (nor the first) to use medical auxiliaries. In fact, such intermediate personnel, with varying titles, are at work in countries as diverse as Bangladesh (basic health worker), Ethiopia (health officer), Fiji (assistant medical officer), Guatemala (rural health technician, health promoter), India (licensed medical practitioner/surgeon's assistant, medical assistant), Kenya, Malawi, New Zealand (doctor assistant), Niger (village health worker), Nigeria, Soviet Union *(feldsher)*, Spain *(practicante)*, Sudan, Tanzania, Uganda, USA (physician's assistant, paediatric nurse practitioner) and Venezuela (nurse auxiliary). The most important recommendation in the use of medical auxiliaries is that they should be recruited and remain in their local districts during both training and later service.

Children's rights What are the priorities where children are concerned? Indeed, what rights do children have anyway? The UN General Assembly in November 1959 adopted the Declaration of the Rights of the Child, in recognition of the need for special safeguards, including legal protection, for children, by reason of their physical and mental immaturity. The Declaration proclaims, among other things, the child's right to healthy growth and development, supported by special care and protection. It further includes adequate prenatal and postnatal care, as well as adequate nutrition, housing, recreation and medical services, with special treatment, education and care for the child who is physically, mentally or socially handicapped. The child should also be protected against neglect, cruelty and exploitation. *All children in less-developed countries fall into the category of those requiring 'special treatment':* the parameters of suffering in the Third World are underlined by disease syndromes that are climate- and environment-related and by problems of transport, water quality and supply, and sanitation in the rural areas.

There are grounds for arguing that the key to the development problem lies first in resolving the complex of problems presented by the needs of children. Consider the significance of only a few of the problem areas in relation to children: food, water and transport, poverty and health, education and human rights. We cannot lay claim to a satisfactory settlement in any of these areas until we have, as a primary obligation, confronted the critical vulnerability of children and secured their future in the context of these special fields of concern. The treatment of the child may be taken as a criterion or yardstick for the degree of success or failure in the working out of social policy, for the effects on children of, in particular, semi-starvation, disease and neglect are frequently not merely harmful, but sometimes irreversible and often fatal. Is this an exaggeration? The fact is that malnutrition, a major problem in African development and one of the greatest causes of disease and death, has its greatest impact on the pre-school child and the mother. Child welfare is vital if we are to achieve a breakthrough in any significant way. Children are of prime and critical importance, for they are the wealth and future of every country.

The human mechanisms involved in these areas are interlocking: it is now as much a matter of fact as of conviction that, for example, reduction in family size is related as much to the quality of life as it is to contraceptive technology. The parallel between the prevention-or-cure antinomy in medical care and the contrast in birth-control policy between the 'silent' factors of child-health quality and the 'saleability' of contraceptive technology is striking. Positive feedback in development will come when life itself is recognized as precious; but when life is cheap, death will be commonplace.

The real cause of death is not always recognized

The killers are silent and insidious: death comes by degrees and the surface drama of disease often only crowns and concludes, but largely obscures, the gradual disintegration produced by protein-energy deficiency and social deprivation. This slow 'social' dying is confronted by indifference by the majority in the rich world:

curative treatment is understood but prevention in this broader sense is not considered the main part of medical care or health policy. The hidden idea behind this is that the 'silent' killers may be ignored, because there is a medical profession and corps available, complete with stethoscope doctors in the traditional white-coat hospital setting. It is assumed that, if there are doctors and hospitals, all is for the best, or heading that way, and that the situation is somehow under control. Actually we know that doctors and hospitals have little to do with health in the larger perspective and in any case are mostly absent from the rural areas of less-developed countries.

In the Western context, most people when they think of health, think of the doctor. The improvement in health that began with the supply of clean water, year-round access to relatively cheap food and adequate housing and clothing has largely been forgotten; sophisticated medical services that came late in the development of the West have been emulated at considerable expense without the prior social engineering having been carried out. As a result, little impact has been made on general well-being by the scarce resources employed.

A further tacit conviction is that death is 'balancing the books': that the dead 'cost nothing'. But is even this true? The wealth of a nation is its people: we must challenge the idea, unspoken but all-pervasive, that death is economically 'necessary'. Has anyone costed death? Or life? Or are we so sensitive that we prefer to hide behind the professional *persona* and take refuge or consolation in medicine that we know is no more than alleviation?

A worsening problem

Of the 1973 African population of some 374 million, infants and children up to 6 years of age constituted about 25 per cent of total population, or, very approximately, 90 million. This age group is proportionally much larger in Africa

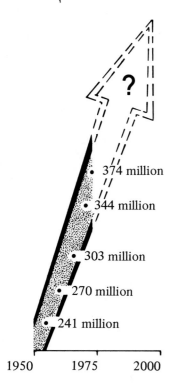

374 million

344 million

303 million

270 million

241 million

1950   1975   2000

Africa's population growth: an exponential line

than it is in the industrialized countries and it is furthermore expected that the number may well double before the century is out. The plight of the children in this category has not yet been given the attention it calls for in national and international development strategies, probably because of the failure hitherto to identify this group of the population as the group that is most at risk (under-reporting of vital statistics, for example, may run from 15 to as high as 50 per cent). But the problems of extending health, nutrition and related services to this increasing number of infants and young children are rapidly becoming serious. The efforts of African governments are often rendered futile by the combination of shortage of resources, transport difficulties, widespread poverty and climatic and other hazards. To make any real impact under such conditions with the limited resources available requires an increasing coordination of the various services and a concerted effort to revise medical personnel and administration criteria for the delivery of public health services.

These problems are of special importance to paediatricians and other doctors caring for children. Paediatrics in the tropics and subtropics has, however, so far tended to give priority to the traditional methods of diagnosis, therapy and prophylaxis within the orthodox medical setting. While much has been achieved in this field, the medical practitioner's share of health care has been too restricted in being limited to the treatment of disease; it is increasingly recognized that the total health of the community depends upon the other 'inputs' that lie outside the sphere of activity of the traditional medical practitioner. This new awareness calls for correspondingly new and integrated interdisciplinary approaches, with a view to formulating action programmes of immediate and practical use, whose object will be to provide every family with a child-care package that will have an optimum effect.

The social and economic consequences of inadequate child care require discussion in a broader context, not only by paediatricians and public-health officials but also by policy-makers and administrators engaged in the overall allocation of economic resources. Hans Singer has suggested that perhaps the most crucial decision that a country has to make is the decision regarding the allocation of resources between the present generation of producers and the future, as represented by its children. 'The more a country is willing and able to spare resources for child development, sufficient to give each individual child a better preparation for life, the higher its chances of achieving a decisive break-away from the vicious circle of poverty and economic stagnation' (Singer, 1972).

The Addis Ababa Seminar

Against this background, the Ethio-Swedish Paediatric Clinic, the Dag Hammarskjöld Foundation and the United Nations Economic Commission for Africa decided to organize the Dag Hammarskjöld Seminar on the Dilemma of Quality, Quantity and Cost in African Child Care, at Addis Ababa, in May 1973. The participants included senior government officials in ministries of public health, social welfare, rural development, finance and planning as well as researchers in these fields, paediatricians and other medical practitioners caring for children. Resource persons were mainly invited from Africa, but also two paediatricians from the People's Republic of China came to address the seminar. An effort was made to obtain the cross-disciplinary collaboration, perhaps for the first time in this field, of participants at varying levels from fields as diverse as social welfare and services, educational psychology, development research and planning, maternal and child health care, curative medicine, economics, rural development and nutrition, with paediatricians and planners, academics, nurses, economists, sociologists and field medical officers.

The optimum package programme

The purpose of the seminar was to try to elaborate the optimum package programme for child care with limited resources. The chain of reasoning that led to this target begins with the recognition of poverty - of the lack of resources adequate to fund a nation-wide general health service - and the need to make the best use of

The Ethio-Swedish Paediatric Clinic (ESPC) was founded in 1957. In 1966, it was made the paediatric department of the medical school, and during recent years it has had an annual turnover of about 2,500 in-patients and 100,000 out-patients.

those resources that are available. The term 'package' embodies the recognition of the multiplier effect: that the impact of concerted delivery of all the inputs is greater than would be the mere total of benefits conferred by individual inputs added together, by consecutive rather than simultaneous implementation for instance. The package concept is therefore more than a fashionable phrase: it is a key idea in the context of resource limitations. The package resolved itself into the following five groups, with all the social inputs entered into the first group (including, somewhat artificially, the socialization process, which in fact represents a dimension to which the other inputs correlate, rather than an element in itself):

Birth

1	PREPARATION OF PARENTS FOR PARENTHOOD	FAMILY WELFARE AND CHILD-SPACING THE SOCIALIZATION PROCESS
2	PERINATAL CARE	
3		NUTRITION IN INFANCY AND CHILDHOOD
4		IMMUNIZATION AND RELATED MEASURES
5	HYGIENE AND ENVIRONMENTAL SANITATION	

Time ➞

Cost considerations were an important concern in preparing for the package. It should be said, however, that there are some false trails in this area and one of these lies in the attempt to take as the point of departure the gain in saving life calculated in money terms, i.e. the cost-benefit approach. It has been shown that cost-benefit calculations, made in terms that require all direct, indirect and intangible benefits to be related to a common monetary base, are already dauntingly difficult to work out in a meaningful or solid way in a western context, even though the technological and statistical apparatus has reached a fair degree of sophistication (Klarman, 1974). This is yet more difficult in the African context, where demographic and other data often have no more value than a sketch. Western economic planning data, as far as health planning is concerned, are themselves in fact rarely tailored to suit the purposes of cost-benefit exercises and usually have to be laboriously reworked from records compiled for other purposes. In the poorer countries there are few exercises in this field. Another reason for this would be the fact that the cost-benefit tools are products of western invention that reflect the degree of development of industrialized societies, in which their utility is more immediately apparent. To this extent they are somewhat culture-bound and belong more to the advanced market economy from which they are derived and in which, it may be argued, cost-benefits criteria in particular are less marginal than what we might call, for want of a better formulation, social-effectiveness criteria.

The lessons of cost analysis

What then is to be learned from cost analysis? The answer lies in the determination of priorities. Cost-effectiveness exercises yield results that may be employed in the planning process, as much at dispensary as at ministerial level. The analysis is invaluable in the design of the package, in order to determine the optimum-impact combination with limited resources. It has to be accepted, of course, that the cost-effectiveness study that is not empirically founded has only a speculative value in that unproven hypotheses or theoretical, non-pragmatic data will not yield results that may be immediately used for policy formation, and this has to be confronted.

We can look at this problem through the hen-and-egg analogy. Which comes first, the hen (empirical study) or the egg (theoretical exercise)? We know that the empirical study is virtually non-existent when we interpret this as rigorously as the total-health concept requires. From the variety of health-programme schemes that are already in operation, there is perhaps not one that uses as its point of departure the integration of all valid health components. The empirical study is therefore only in existence in the form of evaluation of projects that lack comprehensiveness in this sense. At this stage in the debate the priority is therefore upon the need to open up the area of validity for cost-effectiveness studies and this presupposes a prior stage of concentrated conjecture on what is theoretically feasible. If we are to wait for empirical material for policy formulation, we shall not succeed, in the context of the less-developed countries, in generating the interest that is required for imaginative experimentation. The ministerial politician or planner engaged in the daily wrestle with the concrete context is usually not free to engage in the long-range discussion of alternatives in policy and he lacks the analytical material and theoretical formulations that would justify a departure based on anything other than *ad hoc* planning within the framework of increments to existing budget chapters.

This is one justification for the optimum package programme outlined here. It may however be further argued that the optimum package with limited resources is yet another off-the-peg scheme suitable only for the poor: that it therefore represents another, if more refined, substandard offering to those who should also be entitled to basic curative service. It should, therefore, be stated that the demand for curative service from rural populations has to be met in order to make preventive and promotive health inputs accepted. The role of conventional curative work is, however, only partly dealt with here because, in the first place there can be no question of the continuing desirability of standard medical treatment and this has therefore been taken for granted (even though it scarcely exists outside major hospital catchment areas), and in the second place, because the evidence suggests that the main possibility for an improvement in the service lies elsewhere. The medically orthodox approach represents the 'no-change' area and it still commands too large a share of the budget when compared with prevention. This could be altered, however, if the medical profession put some effort into the simplification and social exploitation of the curative work, in order to maintain control over the enormous expansion, both economic and technological, that has resulted from the unnecessary increase in sophisticated variations in the whole field. The lessons here are valid for industrialized countries, especially those such as the United Kingdom that are experiencing a decline in real wealth that is producing a struggle by various interest groups to retain a share of diminishing resources, and countries like the United States that have large masses of the population suffering from poverty and health-care neglect in spite of having developed some impressive therapeutic hardware for the rich.

Family size can only be reduced when the children are likely to survive

The charge of seeking to purvey systems for Africa based on European rather than African values might better be applied to the advocates of crash sterilization or contraceptive-supply programmes, in the family-planning (FP) framework, which receives relatively little consideration in the package programme outlined here. The patent advantages of the FP approach are well known. Levin (1968) calculated, for example, that extended family-planning services to 500,000 women in health-depressed areas of the United States would be about five and a half times as cost effective in reducing annual infant deaths as a programme to provide intensive-care units for high-risk newborn infants. Progress in China is certainly related to the mass-education contraception campaigns waged there. There is a gap, however, between the recognition of the importance of family planning in itself and the possibility of its effective implementation in the actual conditions of the countries of Africa. To illustrate the links in the argument more vividly we may ask whether it will be worth while reducing family size if the children who do remain in the reduced family are still going to die from such a scourge as measles, for example. All too often it is forgotten in the west that family planning is a relatively recent arrival on the scene; the evidence suggests that the implements of family planning only become socially desirable, i.e. that parents will want to use them, when there is reasonable certainty that the children who are born will be able to survive. The fundamental question therefore is not whether FP is desirable in itself but whether it is truly humane or useful for every stage of development. What is needed is to hasten the speed with which the less-developed countries may reach a level of human security at which contraception may be safely taken up by men and women themselves because of its relevance. Family planning implements should certainly be made available, but caution is needed to avoid thrusting techniques upon people that may do no more than add to the debit of human life.

Other elements may be more important than family planning

Less glamorous elements than FP are probably more important in the social component of the package and they may also be cheaper, if not easily calculable in cost-effectiveness terms. Levin's calculations for FP and intensive care (among others) were based on an outlay of US$10 million. Child-spacing teaching, suitably incorporated into the general health programme, might be more remunerative, practically speaking, if the costs were absorbed elsewhere - in the educational budget, for example - by a simple reshaping of present allocations. The importance of such general considerations is growing and, with it, an increasing awareness that if medicine has failed it is because it has fulfilled, in relative isolation, what is essentially a servicing role. Other concepts, other parameters, such as the simple need to feed adequately, have an equally important role to play. There is, for example, an increasing understanding of the infant's need for stimulation from the earliest stage. We have underestimated the importance of cognitive development and its promotion as an essential contributor to the total health of the child.

Parent preparation and the associated considerations represent a relatively new synthesis in health work; not so much a single medical input as a battery of concerns that lie at the edge of, if not outside, the range of activity of the ordinary doctor. They require the collaboration of social workers or cross-cultural experts and it is for this reason that sociologists and educational psychologists were invited to participate in devising the package. The successful programme as a whole can only be created through the mediation of these social considerations, since the overall direction must be determined by the broadest criteria and this is the area of widest social implication. Work in depth is now under way in this field, for example by the Human Ecology Research Station (HERS) at Cali in Colombia, which is seeking to test the hypothesis that 'many of the problems of undernutrition, poor health and underdevelopment of human biological resources (are) interrelated and . . . require more than simple medical solutions' (McKay *et al.*, 1973). The HERS programmes include combinations of nutritional supplementation, health care and psychological stimulation, and are intended to test the belief that food, health care and behaviour stimulation will result in increased capacity to profit from formal education later in the child's life, by a reduction in the intelligence gap, and the more permanently so the earlier the package programme commences in the life of the infant.

The sick child is often out of sight

Where such research schemes sometimes fall down is in their limitation to ᵐⁱⁿⁱnable but restricted age groups, perhaps because of the need to simplify in ord᷄ extrapolate data. It must not be forgotten that the problem of child c᷄ by a failure to comprehend that the bulk of the problem is not easily᷄ child is often out of sight and the volume of unregistered abortions᷄ deaths is nowhere recorded in reliable figures. There is an iceberg-l᷄ the situation, in which the major preoccupation is with the more᷄ elements and with curative methods and their evaluation, which᷄ out because of the definable nature of the medical acts, in term᷄ vaccine utilized, number of medical interventions and so on. ᷄ against childbirth that expresses itself in a primitive belief tha᷄ is intrinsically fraught with danger; that neonatal mortality is u᷄ universal and therefore less amenable to improvement through s᷄

A programme that was designed to reach a stage of self-support (within six years) and that has made considerable progress is the Jamkhed Comprehensive Rural Health Project (Arole & Arole, 1975), in India. The target population of 40,000 comprised some thirty villages; chosen priorities included the attempt to make facilities and personnel available to rural areas, reduction of the high birth rate, an effort to reduce morbidity and mortality in the under-5s and an organized attack on certain chronic illnesses, including notably leprosy and tuberculosis. The success so far achieved is founded upon the concern of the organizers initially to tackle prior social problems, as in the creation of local food and water supplies, and upon the need to recruit local village health workers, who are able to work with the people much more effectively than city-educated staff, who are not always trusted or confided in. A deliberate effort was made by the organizing doctors to prevent curative medicine from dominating the programme, by their allocating their own working time in the following way: 30 per cent to curative services; 30 per cent to public health services; 20 per cent to supervision of other health workers; 10 per cent to training health personnel; and 10 per cent to self-education. The progress made reflects a view of health seen through the eyes of the community rather than of the health professional.

The child-care package should have the widest possible coverage within the limits of available resources and also be of immediate and practical use, and the balance of its content will be determined by analysis of the qualitative, quantitative and cost elements. To assist in these evaluations, a summary of key economic formulations was provided for participants at the Addis Ababa seminar, together with some basic demographic and economic data for a hypothetical developing country, in order to provide a common basis for discussion and analyses. These are printed in the section entitled, 'The Child Care Package'. The parts of the book printed on buff paper correspond largely to the background and lead-up papers and specialist contributions to the seminar. The main section, on white paper, consists of: (1) an outline of the

The sick child is often out of sight

present problem (The Dilemmas), with a selection of contributions to the discussion that followed the presentation of specific examples of dilemmas (The Participants Speak), and an attempt to chart the way towards intermediate solutions (From Perplexity to Progress: The Need to Find a Way Through); (2) the child-care package section itself; (3) and a concluding statement (The Way Forward).

The package section includes a paper written for the book to illustrate the way in which mortality records may be classified, simply and cheaply, for the setting of intermediate goals for the reduction of infant mortality (Degree of Preventiveness in Infant Mortality). It also contains the exploration of three components - perinatal care, nutrition and immunization (Three Studies) - to demonstrate the kinds of rewards made available by cost-effectiveness studies. It is hoped that these exercises will help the health worker with administrative responsibilities to make budget decisions that involve value judgements in the thorny area of medical ethics, in part by helping to bring some better balance into the human muddle that is medicine. They may also encourage those planners who have no medical background to seek the collaboration of professionally trained health staff in order to explore multidisciplinary solutions. The package section is concluded by a resumé of the group discussion on the package components and a final subsection devoted to the problems of weighting the components and of delivering the package.

The difficulty of deriving hard economic data concerning monetary and social benefit from health programme inputs is certainly applicable to hygiene and environmental sanitation. As far as the scale of the improvement is concerned, the evidence is contradictory. It is difficult to evaluate one input in isolation; in one of the few nearly satisfactory studies so far made, water-related disease has been considered of limited importance to adults but of more importance in young children. What must be unquestionable is that the total impact of water-related improvements is very great. The actual increase in world population since the Second World War is itself evidence of the achievement of medical and other inputs on the macro scale, among which must be included hygiene and environmental sanitation. On the micro scale, the doctor treating many diseases in the developing world knows that his present approach and therapy amount to no more than periodic relief of symptoms until mastery over the living environment is also achieved, with all that is implied by adequate supply of good-quality water.

The effort to design an integrated service

The optimum package concept represents the attempt to formulate, at the micro scale, the elements necessary to provide a complete child-specific service, remembering that the child is constantly the first to suffer and often the most difficult to reach. The problem of relative priorities, where most inputs carry an essential character, is dealt with by cross-referencing to more than one social parameter in order to provide a ranking order. The effort to achieve agreement on these interfaces results in an interesting by-product of the discussion: an awareness of the need for all concerned to stop thinking of their professional fields as fortresses to be defended. Somewhere in the ill-defined zone that lies between the closely drawn professional subject areas the child is still suffering. The recent re-thinking about protein requirement, and its repercussions, provides a parallel. Protein requirement has been considerably overestimated and has not been related to the individual's simultaneous energy consumption; nevertheless, further effort to pinpoint the body's precise local requirements might prove highly rewarding in cost-effectiveness terms for a programme that is seeking to maximize effectiveness with limited resources. We should use common sense, of course: the new calorie evaluation may have 'saved' millions of people by reclassifying them as no longer starving, yet people still are dying of hunger, and one periodic extra meal made out of ordinary local products may be better than a 'perfect' nutritional supplement synthesized only after expensive and elaborate effort.

Cross-cultural work is necessary however, since, in the case of economic considerations for example, it is clear that the economic planner is not able to assess health programme needs without some scheme of health priorities produced independently of narrow economic criteria. Otherwise, as Abel-Smith (1972) points out, there is a danger that the economist will only look at the quantifiable (in his terms) elements and ignore the mass of inputs that lie on the periphery of traditionally conceived medical care. A greater degree of cross-disciplinary collaboration is called for if the package is to achieve maximum effectiveness. The relative failure, so far, of the medical package, demonstrates the need for integrated programmes, structured around careful cost-effective evaluations, approaching the problem from the direction of the needs of the community as a whole rather than from the point of view of specialists in isolation. It exposes the extent to which our present medico-educational channels produce 'professionals' whose own élite status and privilege is conducive to class defensiveness and a reluctance to cross the barriers set up by their own specialities. We hope that at some time in the short-term future it will be possible to pursue the work of the Addis Ababa seminar in a practical context, in an effort to transcend these difficulties and to construct the model for a child-care optimum-package programme that will maximize the impact and benefit to be derived from limited resources, to see it working and to be able to evaluate it.

No account of the background to this book would be complete without acknowledging the considerable help given by a number of people at various stages during its production, notably by: Yngve Larsson, who served as the rapporteur of the seminar; Pamela Stilling, for the preparation of the original manuscript; Ante Catipovic, Egon Jonsson and Sarah Macfarlane, for helping to prepare and verify the economic and statistical parts of the book; Delphi Post, for composition of the text for the printer; and Kerstin Kvist, for making the final paste-up.

What is certain above all is that the book would never have been published without the persistent efforts of the General Editor, Sven Hamrell, to persuade his editors to get on with it.

The Background

The Passing Generation

Ernst Michanek

It is customary to speak of the children as 'the coming generation', those who are going to build the future. However, if you study the population statistics, it stands out as a fact that the 'coming' generation could as well be called 'the passing generation'. The majority of those who pass away are children.

Although statistics may sometimes be unreliable, it seems to be the case that in some countries and regions, out of all deaths, not less than 80 per cent occur among children under 5 years of age. In a typical African country, the mortality among these small children may be fifty times higher than in some of the richer countries.

How much human suffering, how much misery do such appalling figures conceal! And how much waste, to speak in economic terms! For we know that a great proportion of this early mortality is unnecessary and in fact easily avoidable. We know this from the experience of recent decades. The present increase in population, which is unparalleled in the history of man and a particular characteristic of the poorer countries, is due not only to an increasing rate of birth but to a decrease in deaths.

Thus, while those who specialize in the economics of development are discussing the widening gap between rich and poor countries and while the danger of famine on a very large scale is growing - at the same time in a number of the poorest countries, in some of the most destitute populations, comparatively great gains have been made, in that there has been a considerable decrease in their infant mortality and an increase in life expectancy.

We all know how some of the most common causes of death have been controlled, how malaria and smallpox and other communicable diseases have been driven back, by the use of insecticides or by vaccination programmes, or through improved water supply or better nutrition, for example. Thanks to modern technology and medicine, in many of the poorer countries of the world or in the poorer sections of national populations, it is not death that has been winning, but human life.

In economic terms, this shows that basic development does not necessarily cost very much. A lot of the waste I have referred to can be quite cheaply avoided - and more savings are obtainable at modest further expense. To put it in a technical way: investment in human resources pays huge dividends, sometimes out of all proportion to the sums invested. Educational campaigns, for example to bring mothers back to the habit of breast-feeding, may require quite marginal expenditures in relation to the gains in human health and happiness.

Some may say - even balanced observers and well-intentioned people - that further prevention of death among children would be futile, since the ensuing fall in the death rate would only add to the more-or-less imminent catastrophe of overpopulation and consequent starvation, that gains today would result in greater losses and human suffering tomorrow.

I belong to those who think that one of the greatest gains for human health and happiness - and for economic and cultural development - will result from a relative decrease in human procreation. Still, my conviction, based on experience, is that the most valid argument against the spacing of children or any form of planned parenthood is the fact that children die. If poor parents do not believe that their offspring will survive - and how can they, from past experience? - they will procreate more. The best argument in favour of restriction in procreation is that children survive.

I repeat: A high rate of sickness and death among infants and children is unnecessary, inhuman and economically wasteful. A further reduction in this kind of human suffering is obtainable and not too expensive.

However, the prospect for the next decades in Africa is that the population of the majority of the countries on the continent will most probably have almost doubled by the end of the century. This increase will present governments with even more severe problems than is now the case - in the provision of proper education for the young, of adequate housing for the families, particularly in the ever more rapidly growing towns, in the organization of useful and gainful employment and in guaranteeing for the population as a whole not only a physical existence but also a quality of life worthy of the twenty-first century.

The costs of nation-building in these circumstances may seem staggering. However, at a relatively modest cost in economic terms, it would be possible to improve immeasurably the quality of childhood and consequently the productive capacity and thus the general well-being of the grown-up members of the next generation. This is particularly true of investment in measures to improve the health of the children.

Such a statement is general enough to be made by someone like myself who is not a child-care expert. When it comes to the question of the precise ways and means to materialize a higher standard of life, not only in economic but also in social and cultural terms as well, in relation to the dilemma of quality, quantity and cost in child care, it is not for me to dogmatize. I am able to make a few observations, however.

Ethiopia was the country with which Sweden started its official development-cooperation programme. Among the first projects on which the two governments agreed to cooperate some twelve to fifteen years ago were some aimed at the building up of facilities for the health and care of children and for staff training, for research into nutrition and for the practical application of its findings. Cooperation had also begun in training and research in construction with a view to improving the housing conditions of the population of Ethiopia, and a programme to build primary schools has now been in operation for over a decade. Whoever created the ideas and drafted the plans, it seems in retrospect that they were wise in choosing activities fundamental for Ethiopia's development into a modern society: the improvement of the basic conditions of life for the coming generation. The choice of fields of activity was based on a tradition of humanitarian activities, undertaken primarily by voluntary agencies; a people-to-people cooperation, as it were, at the grass-roots level.

If I take a more general view of the field of international cooperation for development in the last fifteen years, then it seems that those engaged in development work have only lately agreed to emphasize in actual practice the social aspects of development. Government budgets of developing countries, which, of course, play the greatest role for their development as well as so-called aid programmes, were for a long time characterized by a strong preference for projects that would enhance development in economic terms, those, that is, likely to add to the growth of the gross national product. After national security and defence, which are still given first priority in most countries, measures conducive to the development of an infrastructure in industry and foreign trade have played a dominant role. The distribution of an increasing national income has as a rule not been in focus: the equalization of opportunity has been paid more attention in the development plans than in actual practice.

It must immediately be admitted, however, that in many national development budgets, education has taken an increasing share as the numbers of children and young people have grown - and indeed, the standard of health is also raised by improved educational standards. But the educational systems of many developing countries have been based on western concepts and models and they have not been adequately geared to the most pressing needs for knowledge and skills in the primarily rural economies of the countries concerned. Educational organization and methods have been ill-adapted to the actual conditions of these countries. In spite of all efforts, the number of illiterates in the world is still increasing, numbering today some 800 million adults, probably about 100 million more than twenty years ago. Unemployment is increasing to appalling proportions among the unskilled - and to some extent also among those who have received training, because their training has not been geared to the potentials and needs of the national economies.

In the field of health and medical services great progress has taken place, but in most countries the rural masses have so far not been adequately cared for and organization and training have as a rule not been adapted to the conditions of the people they should serve. The medical training system used at Gondar in Ethiopia may be quoted as one of the good, early examples of a technique adapted to local conditions; at the same time it does not seem as if the considerable means employed in central health installations have given the dividends they were hoped to give, either for the capital city or for the country as a whole. The concentration of health facilities in the towns has aggravated the inequality between rural and urban areas; it has also contributed to the influx of people into the towns and aggravated the social problems there.

In development cooperation, over the last ten years it has become an accepted principle that the programming of activities supported from outside should be in the hands of the national governments. They must set the priorities for their own development: they are the ones who will have the responsibility for the proper implementation of the plans and it is they who will, immediately or in the long run, carry the bulk of the costs.

In my experience, requests for foreign assistance to programmes of a clearly social character have been slow in coming forward. Although ministers of health, for instance, may personally have pressed the foreign aid agencies for support, the planning and finance ministries, which play a leading role in the selection of priorities for foreign aid, have not given the same weight to investments in human resources as to other investments. I am afraid that this attitude in general has been shared by both the so-called recipient and donor governments. The economic growth targets have been in the forefront on both sides.

The result has been that in such fields as health and nutrition, partly also in education, a great deal of the international cooperation has been left to non-governmental forces. Voluntary agencies have played a very important role with enthusiasm and skill for the provision of health services - but they have had neither the funds nor the ability to build national networks based on comprehensive plans; and again the rural areas have not been adequately provided for.

My personal background is a country that has reached a comparatively high level of GNP *per capita* and high standards in regard to infant survival, child health, literacy and life expectancy - and a low birth rate achieved by an entirely voluntary restriction of childbearing. I am biased, of course, by my former association with the national administration in the field of social affairs, housing and labour. None the less, it does not seem surprising to me that great public expense for child care, health, social security, rehabilitation of the handicapped and housing - and of course, for all kinds of education and training - in my own country coincides with

high individual income standards and with a distribution of income that seems to be less uneven than in most countries. I believe that some of the main reasons for this state of affairs are: (a) the build-up of a public health service throughout the country, which some would label a system of socialized medicine but which was in fact first organized between 200 and 300 years ago, that is, in a totally rural economy; (b) the introduction of compulsory primary education more than 100 years ago, that is, before the industrialization and urbanization of the country really began; (c) a structure of local government and of local taxation, again with roots in ancient history, which fostered initiative and responsibility at the village level.

It is because of this personal experience that I am convinced that the governments of the world were right, when they all agreed, five years ago, on the International Development Strategy for the United Nations Second Development Decade, in which the following statement is to be found: 'As the ultimate purpose of development is to provide increasing opportunities to all people for a better life, it is essential to bring about a more equitable distribution of income and wealth for promoting both social justice and efficiency of production, to raise substantially the level of employment, to achieve a greater degree of income security and to expand and improve facilities for education, health, nutrition, housing and social welfare, and to safeguard the environment. Thus, qualitative and structural changes in the society must go hand in hand with rapid economic growth, and existing disparities - regional, sectoral and social - should be substantially reduced. These objectives are both determining factors and end results of development: they should therefore be viewed as integrated parts of the same dynamic process, and would require a unified approach.' The statement specified, among other things, that each developing country should formulate a coherent health programme for the prevention and treatment of diseases and to raise the general level of health and sanitation with improved nutritional levels that place special emphasis on the needs of vulnerable groups of the population. It also specifies that the well-being of children should be fostered.

International declarations may be looked upon as mere words - and in fact I feel rather critical towards the United Nations system for not having emphasized stronger and earlier the particular role of child care and other measures for children and mothers. However, as we are now beginning to get an international code of conduct concerning social development activities, these declarations are there to be used to create and foster public opinion and to help us in exerting pressure on public authorities in each country. There are other declarations and strategies from various United Nations bodies - from Unicef, WHO, FAO and other international bodies - but we need more action-oriented programmes and plans, directed notably towards the improvement in various respects of the status of girls and women in our societies, who carry a particular burden in regard to the children. The international discussion over the last few years on the social goals of development has helped to pave the way for a stronger emphasis on the kind of programmes discussed below, both in national and in international planning and budgeting. In bilateral development cooperation we have been happy to see more requests in recent years for international cooperation in these fields, and the assistance programmes have to some extent reflected this new direction.

Recent upheavals on the international scene - world inflation, the energy crisis and the problem of recycling the wealth produced by the redistribution of income from oil resources, growing unemployment and increasing scepticism about debt-financing of development, together with the growing food shortage - have contributed to produce a state of turmoil. The conviction is growing that a radically new direction is called for in the United Nations system, a direction that will not merely be expressed by the production of further tons of documents and the reshuffling of agency structures.

One thing is clear: that the change that anybody may advocate in order to obtain what they consider to be progress must rest upon the values and traditions of each particular society and start from there, building the effort to change upon the conviction and cooperation of those immediately concerned.

This means that proposals for action should deal primarily with down-to-earth activities that can influence the grass-roots and thereby the daily lives of the weak and vulnerable personalities with whose well-being and welfare we are here concerned - the children, the majority of our peoples, who are the least privileged among the underprivileged in the world today.

In our discussion on child welfare policies we often quote the phrase, 'All children should be welcome children'. Society and economy should be so organized that not only the family but also the community can welcome all children who are born and so that the children themselves may really feel that they are not being looked on as a gift or as a burden only but as individuals with the rights of citizens in a better, more prosperous world. This should be a motto for planners as well as health workers, for central administrators and field staff alike.

The View of the Economic Planner

Oscar Gish

Solutions to the child-care problem cannot be generated in the abstract, without reference to existing institutions and institutional methods. Oscar Gish here discusses, from the point of view of the budget planner, the general problem of delivering health services.

Planning, Plans and Planners

In most Third World countries (as in most others) it is usual for the national budget to be determined by the ministry of finance in keeping with overall national priorities and in negotiation with the various ministries. These budgeting procedures are undertaken each year and usually fall within the context of a larger multi-year plan. Although most developing countries now prepare five-year-type plans, in practice most of these plans have a marked tendency to run out of steam after the first year or two. This is a reflection of the fact that the governments involved are unable to define and control their futures beyond that one or two years. What happens then is that the annual plan or annual budget becomes in fact the only 'plan' that has any true meaning: of course, such situations to a substantial degree negate the very concept of planning, which requires longer periods of time than one year for the planning and implementation of programmes of work.

Some of the problems standing in the way of successful planning have certainly stemmed from the inability of many planners to separate fact from fancy. For example, a great fuss has been made of cost-benefit analyses as an instrument of planning; however, in connexion with health-service planning at least, grave problems arise in attempting to utilize this device. In a cost-benefit analysis, as applied to health services, the benefits are usually calculated as being the cumulative earnings that will accrue to individuals (and indirectly to governments) whose lives have been extended or whose level of morbidity has been reduced as a result of particular health investments (costs). In a rather more sophisticated system the benefits might be calculated as the additional physical output resulting from the labour of the additional years of life or better physical condition (health) that has been granted to the 'saved' worker. In this system the value of the additional output is determined in terms of the market price of the product on the same basis as the additional earnings of the worker would have been calculated (some theoretical work has attempted to apply economic rather than market value to outputs - however, rarely if ever has this type of analysis been applied, at least in the health sector). The difficulty with this method of calculation is that if at the same moment there were to be thrown on to the labour market all of those who are at any particular time ill, or all of those whose lives would be saved as a result of particular health-service inputs, it would then be necessary to recalculate the whole of the value of economic output. This is so just because the particular market values attached to any volume of output are based precisely upon prevailing economic conditions, and such significant changes as would come about as a result of massive numbers of workers suddenly becoming available to the labour market would drastically change those values.

Even more important is that in conditions such as exist in most of the Third World, with its very great volume of unemployment and underemployment, it is impossible to calculate even theoretically what would happen if suddenly there were many more working lives added to the labour market. Even if such calculations have relevance in the conditions of relatively full employment, that is, in industrialized countries enjoying levels of unemployment that now generally run at only 2 to 5 per cent of the labour force (discounting the current recession), in most Third World countries where there is a lack of wage employment and productive agriculture and very substantial levels of unemployment and underemployment it is impossible to predict what value of additional output would actually occur from a saved life. Thus this particular cost-benefit methodology has very severe limitations attached to it when attempted in the context of the realities of Africa, Asia and Latin America.

Another serious problem in applying cost-benefit analyses in the context of many countries and most particularly in the Third World is that the costs and benefits under discussion do not accrue to the same families or social strata within national societies. For example, the costs of raising a child are borne primarily by the family and not by the state or any other specific organs of the national society; however, many of the inputs necessary to have saved a child's life would not be primarily borne by the family but by the state through its ministry of health, or water development, or education, for example. The problem is that in many if not most governments, decision-making is controlled by those whose immediate interests lie elsewhere than in the prevention of infant deaths in general. This happens even though those families that are suffering from the highest levels of infant mortality are also likely to be contributing important resources to the governmental structure, because they are little represented in that structure when decisions about resource allocation are being taken. This is the crux of the problem and, unfortunately, it is highly unlikely to surface within the context of very many cost-benefit analyses.

In the advanced, industrialized (non-collectivized) countries there exist more or less progressive income-tax structures which have as their purpose the transfer of resources from those who have managed to take more out of the social system to those who have managed to take less; the instrument of transfer being the state through its tax structure. If such governments attempt to increase their possibilities for putting additional resources into the control of infant deaths, without correspondingly reducing other government allocations, they increase the volume of taxes passing through their (progressive) tax systems. What this means, of course, is that those who are suffering the least from infant mortality, i.e. the upper levels of society, are required to make a greater contribution to the saving of other people's infants, that is, those at the base of society. Thus, if cost-benefit analyses are to make any sense at all, they need at the very least to relate benefits to costs in terms of specific groups. In any event, very few governments ever actually carry out formal cost-benefit analyses in regard to health-sector developments (although the appearance of such exercises may be gone through to satisfy an aid donor). None the less, academic health planners continue stressing the need for cost-benefit analyses, thereby diverting attention away from more fruitful lines of exploration.

All of this is not to argue that there are not costs and benefits attached to particular programmes and projects. Of course there are, but their proper methods of calculation are quite different from those being utilized in conventional cost-benefit analyses. In any event, it is also quite certain that most of the basic decisions that now need to be taken in connexion with health-service development are relatively simple and do not require very complex mathematical quantification. This is so because existing health-care systems have been allowed to become so extremely inefficient that even a relatively small amount of applied common sense would carry them very far in a more rational direction. What would be most useful would be to carry out *basic cost-effective studies* of alternative methods of providing health-care services.

These cost-effectiveness studies would be of assistance not least of all because they could become a powerful tool in the hands of any decision-maker truly wanting to change the inappropriate pattern of health services that is now so commonly seen. There is also the consideration that during the confused period when budgets are actually under preparation, a time during which decisions have to be made very quickly, anyone with specific figures to offer is in a better position to have their particular projects approved. It is the case that ministries of health have been notoriously weak in being able to present to development planners in ministries of finance well-thought-out arguments in favour of improved allocations for the health sector. Planning and projects based upon simple cost-effective studies could strengthen those arguments.

In the past, very much so-called health planning has been left to the academic public health doctor: all too often such planners have too little knowledge of the ways in which planning and budgeting is actually done by governments. It is insufficiently appreciated that ministries allocate against specified facilities and programmes, so that proposals being made for new plans must follow from current budgetary allocations and structures. If, for example, a new cadre of manpower is being proposed it must fit into an employment pattern at some already existing type of facility, or into some that will be created. In addition this cadre must have a clear-cut career and wage structure which bears an appropriate relationship to all those already in employment, at least within the ministry of health if not in the nation as a whole.

However, for better or worse, the academic planners are having little immediate effect on the actual pattern of resource allocation within most Third World ministries of health. Decision-making is being influenced primarily by senior members of the medical profession, with the clinical specialists playing a quite disproportionate role. The situation varies in keeping with the complexity of the decision-making structure. In Africa the clinical specialists are most powerful, not least of all because of the very small size of their profession: if those few surgeons or pathologists, etc. who make up the profession agree on the next steps to be taken in relationship to their own areas of medical expertise, there is likely to be no opposition. The fact that the size of the profession in Africa is so small also means that very many of the doctors were together at medical school and have not as yet divided along functional job lines.

Health planning
The discussion here is concerned with the development of health services and not 'health' itself, presupposing that the provision of certain kinds of health services will in time affect health, as such.

The health plan generally represents that part of a plan document which sets out the work to be undertaken by a ministry of health. It must be recognized that the work of the ministry of health as such represents only a small part of the entire plan that has very close and immediate bearing upon the health of populations: the 'creation' of health comprises a great deal more than is likely to result from an expansion of the volume of services conventionally offered by the ministry of health. For example, the World Health Organization has defined health as a state of complete physical, mental and social well-being. Obviously such a state cannot be achieved only through the work of ministries of health. Even if, instead, the aim were a much simpler and potentially realizable goal it would still be necessary to recognize the integrated nature of health-creating plans. Obviously the activities of ministries of water, agriculture, education and others will have at least as much bearing upon the health of a population as that of just the ministry of health.

In any event it is likely that there will be a close correlation in any one country between the sorts of planning to be found in the health sector and the kinds of planning to be found in those other sectors having a bearing upon health. For example, if a national health planning system is primarily based upon the construction of a handful of very large urban hospitals it also may be expected that water-development schemes will be largely concentrated in the towns; conversely, it can be expected that a ministry of health which is specifically planning to serve the mass of the population will find it necessary to gear its planning work to the provision of services to the countryside and to the selective development of urban services that are more likely to be utilized by that part of the town population in the lower socio-economic groupings, and such planning would require a significant shift of resources from hospital and other urban services to the rural areas. In order to accomplish the latter there would need to be a very drastic slowing down of hospital building in virtually any Third World country; it might even be necessary to stop absolutely further hospital building for a considerable period of time. The usual medical reaction to such suggestions is that it is the task of the ministry of finance to provide ministries of health with resources adequate enough to create a 'good' health system, i.e. one that is sufficiently comprehensive so as to reach the whole of the rural population as well as to continue to provide large specialized hospital services. Unfortunately, it is not possible to create an acceptable rural health infrastructure, given the very inadequate services that now exist, without turning the limited available resources very sharply towards the countryside. ...

In fact, the clearest road ahead exists in those countries in which the budget of the ministry of health is growing and at a reasonable rate, say 5 to 8 per cent per annum in real terms; such a rate of increase could, broadly speaking, provide in perhaps a decade an acceptable rural health infrastructure in very many if not most countries of the Third World, provided that virtually the whole of the increase was to be applied to the development of that rural health infrastructure. In those countries where ministry of health budgets are growing at less than the 5 to 8 per cent indicated above it might be possible to convince governments to raise health-sector allocations in response to plans intended to expand rapidly the rural health infrastructure. Governments are becoming increasingly concerned at the lack of rural health services and plans for the urgent extension of such services so they might be amenable to this sort of planning. If treasury people were assured that there would in fact be a spread of health services throughout the countryside and that additional health-sector expenditure would not lead to the construction of yet another big urban hospital it is quite possible that they could be won over to support increased expenditure for the health sector.

Making the health plan

In the making of a multi-year health plan the disease pattern can usually be taken as given, i.e. there is no great need for extensive epidemiological work before proceeding with the plan. This is so just because the existing pattern of health services departs so drastically from the disease situation as it is already known to be. There is now in virtually every Third World country far more information about the pattern of disease than is being used in the actual health plan and resource allocation processes. Of course, as resource allocation in the health sector comes closer to reflecting the known disease patterns it will become necessary to extend the volume of data available to the health planner. The imbalance between available data and the areas in which still more data is being sought and the kinds of data that are actually required for planning reflects the lack of reality in planning mentioned earlier. Clearly, it will not be possible to create useful health plans until more data are available that relate to the existing pattern of resource allocation and resource utilization in the health sector. Fortunately, most of what is required could be readily made available. We need to know in some detail just how money, manpower and facilities are being utilized and just how effective services are in reaching the whole of the population. It is also necessary to know much more about the costs of specific types of services and the benefits accruing from those services. In this connexion it is worth noting that although ministries of health generally do collect data on expenditure and utilization of services these are not assembled for planning purposes but remain within the context of their original administrative function. It is necessary to make these data explicit in regard to health-service development. This is even more crucial for activities related to children. With the assembly of basic data on costs and utilization it is then possible to proceed with the health plan. The point of departure must be the recurrent budget; it is this budget that is likely to be a greater constraint upon development than the capital budget, especially if future development is to be primarily centred in the countryside rather than in large urban institutions. If the growth rate of the recurrent health budget is known then it becomes possible to estimate the volume of that budget at some future point in time, say the end of the next five-year plan. Once that figure is known it is possible to determine how it will be spread across the items making up the areas of expenditure of a ministry of health, i.e. national, provincial and district hospitals, rural health centres and health stations, preventive programmes, manpower training, administration, and so on. The present distribution of the budget in these various areas will be known and appropriate targets for the end of the next plan could then be set out in keeping with possible rates of change. The major direction of that change would be away from hospital expenditures and towards small rural units, preventive health campaigns and training. (At the moment most Third World countries spend perhaps two-thirds or more of their health budget for hospital services; health centres and subcentres take between 10 and 20 per cent; and the final 10 to 15 per cent of the budget is distributed in administration, training and preventive programmes.) The plan itself would be based upon the known costs of additional facilities and programmes. Thus if it is known that the average cost of running a regional hospital bed is x, then it can be calculated that an additional 26 beds at such an institution will cost roughly $26x$ to operate. If such exercises are worked through for each of the planned new facilities and programmes it then becomes possible to fit it all together within the constraint of the size of the expected recurrent budget at the end of the plan period. There are relatively few basic figures required for such an exercise, which makes it all the more surprising that so few ministries

have managed to provide those that are required. One reason for this is certainly that the limited capacity of statistical departments within ministries of health is largely taken up with the collection of disease statistics (which are seldom put to any practical use). Another is the fact that statistics and accounts are kept primarily for administrative purposes, in forms that are not particularly useful for planning.

The capital budget may be called the mother of the recurrent budget, in that the money spent now for new facilities and training programmes will determine the future recurrent budget. The shape of the capital budget over one or two five-year plans can dramatically change the recurrent budget by the end of that period. The capital budget of a ministry of health is likely to be largely made up of expenditure on buildings, but it is important to stress that buildings alone are certainly not the key to health service development. It is certainly the case that appropriate staffing represents a much more significant aspect of health service development than does the mere provision of buildings.

Health manpower planning

Employment costs will take around half the total budget of a ministry of health. The salaries of health workers will comprise roughly half to two-thirds of that and the balance will cover the wages of domestic and other such ancillary staff. The major constraint to expansion of the number of health workers in ministry employment will be the size of the recurrent budget. Health workers, however, fall into many different categories and levels and thus offer a varied mix of employment possibilites. Health manpower is most conveniently divided into vertical and horizontal groupings. The vertical divisions follow fairly distinct, traditional areas of work, e.g. medical practitioners, nurses, laboratory workers, etc. Horizontal divisions, in turn, separate these vertical groupings into different levels of training and skill. The top level comprises the internationally recognized types of professionals - the medical doctor, the state-registered nurse and so on. Many Third World countries have a second tier, below the professional level, which can be termed the technician level. These health workers comprise those with ten to twelve years of schooling followed by a two to three years of training. In addition to the two levels described above, some Third World countries have a third, auxiliary level made up of those with primary-school education (usually of six to eight years) followed by one to two years of training.

Given the number of possible mixes of different sorts of health workers, the question becomes one of choosing that mix which comes closest to meeting the total national requirement for health workers. To that end there must be two starting-points: one, the resolve to cover the whole of the country with a network of health services including the manpower to staff those services; two, explicit recognition of the financial constraint that exists as a barrier to unlimited staff expansion. Recognition of the economic constraint makes rational planning possible; we are then able to calculate the training and employment costs of alternative types of manpower, e.g. one registered medical doctor or some significantly larger number of medical assistants. (In practice the trade-off, in Africa at least, between such different sorts of medical practitioners is likely to run to fifteen or twenty medical assistants, or perhaps double that number of rural medical aides, at the cost of one conventional medical doctor.) Of course, the decisions as to numbers of specific types and levels of health workers must be related to the different kinds of health facilities to be developed in the country. Since it is in practice more likely that manpower development will prove to be a greater bottleneck than supply of facilities (buildings), it is the manpower plan that should determine the facilities rather than the other way round.

It is important to stress that in planning health manpower there is no need to accept any fixed ratios of staff to facilities, or staff to other types of staff. The appropriate mix will vary with the economic possibilities of the country for training and employing people, the supply of candidates for particular levels of training, the number of training institutions and teachers, and so on. What is likely to be the case virtually everywhere in health-manpower development is that some sort of pyramidal shape should be aimed for, thus if a country has three levels of medical practitioner there should be one registered doctor to two or more medical assistants, to a still greater number of medical aides.

The setting in Africa of the well-advertised doctor-to-population target of 1 to 10,000 has helped to do a great deal of damage to sensible health-manpower planning in the continent - as similar targets have done in other places. This ratio has long been an established target and although other types of staff-to-population targets may exist they are referred to rarely, if ever. In practice the one target that is known to all is used as a means of justifying ever larger investments for the production of doctors, even in the absence of any adequate levels of training for various types of doctor-auxiliary or other classes of health manpower. In practice there is no justification for such targets - doctors do not work in relationship to population but in relationship to health-service facilities. Thus it may be possible to say that a hospital of so many beds should have a minimum of so many doctors, or that there will be one doctor acting in a supervisory capacity to x number of health centres, or that specific public-health campaigns will require so many doctors to run them, and so on; but to put a doctor into the middle of a population of 10,000 in the absence of any particular facility would obviously make no sense at all. In addition, to discuss total numbers of doctors to population in the absence of any consideration of the way the doctors are distributed is to ignore the realities of this problem in almost all countries. It is already the case that many large cities in the Third World are enjoying a doctor-to-population ratio that is equivalent to overall doctor-population ratios in the industrialized countries. Even in Africa in some large cities there is nearly one doctor for every thousand inhabitants, although in those same countries it is also possible to find regions and provinces containing hundreds of thousands of people that have resident in them not more than one, two or three doctors.

In practice, in Africa the 1 to 10,000 doctor-population ratio has become an instrument for pressuring governments into allocating more resources to the production of doctors. However, it needs also to be noted that many of these same governments would in any event have had their own internal reasons for wanting to increase the number of doctors in the country, even at the price of having extremely unbalanced health manpower outputs. None the less, although it is being argued here that there are no sacred manpower-to-population or manpower-to-health-facility ratios, there are some ratios that are better and some that are worse and, at a given moment, when preparing a health manpower plan it is necessary to think in terms of some sort of ratios that will hold at least until the end of the planning period. The ratios that are to be established cannot be chosen arbitrarily, nor

must they be drawn from more economically advanced countries (which has certainly proved to be disastrous). Some of the basic issues involved in establishing ratios, such as national coverage and acceptance of economic constraints, have been discussed above. In addition there is the need to take into account the economic concept of a division of labour leading to increased productivity and the managerial concept of appropriate delegation of authority. Such concepts lead clearly to the increased use of lower-level manpower for many of the less sophisticated tasks that now occupy so much of the time of highly trained professional manpower.

There ought to be no need to belabour the argument in favour of the use of many more auxiliaries than is now commonly the case. Enough has been said about the matter in recent years to convince all who have given serious thought to the question (except, of course, those with opposing institutional interests). It is probably fair to say that opposition to the use of greater numbers of medical assistants and other doctor-auxiliaries stems mainly from professional and elitist interests, and almost verges on the irrational; at least, in terms of the health-care requirements of the mass of population in poor countries this opposition is certainly irrational. . . .

In making the health-manpower plan there are a number of bits of technical data that need to be known. For example, we need to know just how many health workers of each category and level are now in employment within the country, also who their employers are and (where possible) the wastage rate from professional employment. In addition we need details of the wage structure of the different health-manpower cadres; that is, the costs involved in their employment. In the sphere of training, information on the capacity of the training institutions in terms of students and teachers, the wastage rate from training and the costs of that training is required. These data are not ordinarily very difficult to obtain: any reasonably well-organized ministry of health could gather them, at least for their own employees and institutions. If there is a large private sector involved in health-manpower employment - and perhaps even training - the problem could become rather more complex, but in African countries, because of the small initial base and overall importance of government activities in the health sector, health-manpower surveys and projections can be made more easily. For the purposes of the health-manpower plan, in addition to the manpower statistics indicated above, there will be need for estimates as to the size of the recurrent budget, the building plan and the preventive-health campaigns that are to be developed. These data too should be relatively easily available to ministries of health and taken together with the specified manpower data are sufficient for the creation of a proper manpower plan. . . .

Ministries of health or ministries of disease?

In many respects ministries of health in most of the world might more correctly be termed ministries of disease. This can be said because ministries of health as we mainly know them are capable of doing relatively little in relationship to health itself, instead they primarily provide services for those already suffering from disease. It is probably the case that ministries of health could do considerably more about health, as opposed to disease, than they are now doing, but it is also probably true that the bulk of health inputs, as opposed to anti-disease inputs, are in fact beyond the scope of their conventional activities. There are two reasons for this. One is that the major factors influencing human health are related to the services provided by such ministries as agriculture or education, rather than ministries of health. The other reason is that good health is not a service provided by governments (in the conventional sense) at all; people basically 'do for themselves' with regard to their own health requirements. Of course, governments and ministries may help to create the circumstances in which people can better help themselves, but they cannot substitute for the direct actions of people. It may be that ministries of health can best facilitate the development of the health of national populations (a) by being supportive of the physical and social environmental needs of (particularly rural) populations as they are now being met by other ministries than health and (b) by helping to create conditions which allow people to care for themselves in a health-promoting way.

The implications of such an approach to health are of course very far-reaching. It means a departure from the (implicitly) accepted engineering and technological approach to health development. It also means that decision-making in the health sector must become part of the explicit subject-matter of political economy. This is not to imply a totally negative approach to the possibilities of even conventionally organized ministries of health, for there is certainly much that they can now do even within the constraints under which they operate (some of the possibilities have been indicated above); none the less, the limitations are real.

It is at the village level itself that the best possibilities exist for rapid progress in health development. There is probably no ministry of health in Africa that knows how to create a genuine, locally based health service and over the world there are very few examples of such services. Reports suggest that in the People's Republic of China substantial progress has been made in this direction. In many countries there is talk of providing village-level services through the planned activities of government. Such efforts are to be supported but they beg the question of what government schemes can actually do in helping villagers to fulfil their own health-care requirements. It may very well be that the source of so much failure in the health sector stems precisely from this point, in that government planners either do not have as much wisdom and skill as is generally thought to be the case or that this wisdom and these skills are not very relevant to local/village-level problems. There can be little doubt that villagers have the potential, if not the existing capacity, to organize their own lives in such a way as to produce sufficient skills to do most of that which is required to create a healthy life environment. The proviso is that there should exist a form of social organization at the national level that, at the very least, is not destructive of the possibilities of self-reliant village development. Unfortunately most ministries (not only of health) are not only incapable of giving the kind of support needed at village level but are themselves part of larger national structures that are actually destructive of the possibilities of self-reliant village development.

The general problem under discussion can be illustrated in the context of manpower development. The usual thing is for ministries of health to train personnel who then join the civil service and draw wages on a monthly basis; however, there are obvious limitations to the current possibilities of civil servants when dealing with the immense health-care problems that exist in African and other Third World countries. What is required, rather, is a sense of participation on the part of village populations, including those selected for specific health-care activities. Of course such participation can become a real possibility only in the context of nations that have organized themselves in keeping with the needs of the whole of the population. What is needed are people in each village who know something about the environmental health-care needs of their fellow villagers; such people should come from the village and remain part of its day-to-day functioning. There is no way to put the large number of people that is required for such work on to ministerial payrolls; therefore, they must continue to make their livelihoods from within the village itself. Preferably they will continue to have the possibility to grow their own food while being recompensed from community resources for the time they spend at their health-work activities. Some will recognize here the Chinese concept of the so-called 'barefoot doctor'. This is not to recommend that others follow what has been done in another country, but the basic principle of drawing health workers from the community itself does remain valid. However, the real problem is not merely to envisage some sort of 'ideal' structure but to make recommendations for the accomplishment of that particular structure in the context of societies that are geared towards money wages, career promotions and escape from the village to the city. The question of how to create alternative sorts of motivations for both national leaders and villagers remains probably the most important issue for future social and economic development, in both the general sense as well as when applied specifically to health and health services.

OTHER PUBLICATIONS

1. *Doctor Migration and World Health: The Impact of the International Demand for Doctors on Health Services in Developing Countries.* London, Bell, 1971.
2. *Health Manpower and the Medical Auxiliary: Some Notes and an Annotated Bibliography.* London, Intermediate Technology Development Group, 1971. (General éditor.)
3. Resource Allocation, Equality of Access, and Health. *Int. J.Hlth Serv.,* Vol.3, No.3, Summer 1973. (Reprinted in *Wld Dev.,* Vol.1, No.12, December 1973.) This paper was first delivered at the Addis Ababa Seminar, on 14 May 1973.
4. Doctor Auxiliaries in Tanzania. *Lancet,* 1 December 1973.
5. Ujamaa, The Way Forward. *Wld Hlth,* April 1975.
6. *Planning the Health Sector: The Tanzanian Experience.* London, Croom Helm. (In press.)

Integrated Training for Total Health Care

G. L. Monekosso

Public-health policies have been hindered in their implementation by the emphasis upon structures and specialities rather than upon personnel and general abilities. Professor Monekosso discusses the priority need for adequate training of personnel in the total health concept, if the optimal solution to the child health problems is to be achieved, with less emphasis upon ideal plans that cannot be executed, for lack of resources, and more upon the defined needs of specific communities.

The administrative and political context

Many African countries define their health policy as follows: total coverage of the whole population, with preventive medicine as the priority. Some in addition believe in integrating health care, with preventive, curative and social aspects organized as one major effort, rather than in separate watertight compartments.

One observes quite often a health-care pyramid, at the top of which is a national reference centre (this may also be the university hospital) - a centre that ideally should combine specialized clinical, laboratory and public-health activities in one integrated 'summit'. Countries with populations of 5 million or less and favourable geographical and socio-economic factors could manage with only one reference centre. Larger countries may require several. Next there are provincial hospitals (and associated preventive-medicine centres) each serving up to 1 million inhabitants; then there are district hospitals which often cater for some 150,000 to 250,000 people; and finally districts may be subdivided into communes each of which is served by a small hospital or developed health centre for its 20,000 or more people. One observes a decreasing order of complexity as one goes down the pyramid, from the national, regional or state reference centre, through the provincial or district hospitals to the health centres (or cottage hospitals) of the communes. In an African country with over 5 million inhabitants one may find one or two reference centres, five to ten provincial hospitals, up to forty district hospitals and perhaps 200 developed health centres or small 'cottage' hospitals.

This is the usual administrative context in which 'total health care' is delivered to the population of many African countries. Owing to budgetary limitations, shortage of trained staff and lack of an adequate infrastructure, governmental and other organized health care is only theoretically 'total'. It is now increasingly realized that properly trained personnel in adequate numbers is indispensable and may be quite crucial in resolving the dilemma of quality, quantity and cost in health-care delivery.

Categories of health personnel

Because of the very low *per capita* expenditure on health in many tropical countries, we can only aim at satisfying the most fundamental health needs of the people. The Addis Ababa seminar identified seven elements necessary in a comprehensive package programme for African child health care. The categories of personnel for the relevant health-care tasks would seem to be as follows:

Preparation of parents for parenthood: social-welfare workers, psychologists and experienced clinical workers (nurse-midwives or physicians).

Family welfare and child-spacing: primary-care physicians, nurse-midwives, social-welfare workers, etc.

The socialization process: medical sociologists or anthropologists, medical psychologists, social-welfare workers, rehabilitationists, etc.

Perinatal care: primary-care physicians, nurse-midwives, paediatric-nurse practitioners, paediatricians, obstetrician-gynaecologists.

Nutrition in infancy and childhood: community-health physicians, paediatricians, nutritionists and dietitians.

Immunization and related measures: community-nurse practitioners, health inspectors, public-health physicians, etc.

Hygiene and environmental sanitation: sanitary engineers

sanitary/environmental technicians, laboratory technicians. This list of categories of health personnel is not exhaustive. It does not include the highly specialized personnel to whom difficult problems are referred or the health auxiliaries to whom quite important functions are delegated. The health personnel are therefore regrouped as follows:

Group A. Senior health professionals: physicians, specialized physicians, senior nurse practitioners, superintendent technical personnel, senior medico-social personnel.

Group B. Health professionals: nurse practitioners (many types), health technicians (many types), medico-social workers, specialized health professionals (many types).

Group C. Health auxiliaries: junior technicians, junior field assistants, etc.

This classification allows a rational planning of multi-professional training programmes, in such a manner as to facilitate the constitution of health teams capable of efficiently coping with defined health-care delivery programmes.

Multiprofessional training institutions

Traditionally, health personnel are trained in separate institutes: medical schools, nursing schools, radiography, physiotherapy, medical assistant and nursing-aid schools, etc. The last half-century has seen the development of large 'medical centres' or university medical centres. These are complex multiprofessional establishments including several administratively autonomous institutions, sharing only one common facility: the university hospital. The latter is also the focal point of interest since these medical centres concentrate on 'curative' activities. Emphasis on preventive medicine is minimal. Teaching programmes - for medical students, nurses, technicians, and so on - are organized in watertight compartments; even their practical assignments in the university hospital are organized separately.

Some university centres for health sciences have broken through this barrier. All teaching programmes are planned together and wherever possible theoretical, laboratory, clinical and field assignments are shared by students of the different health professions; there is also an important emphasis on public health and close links with the public health service of their country. Committed to work as members of health teams, they study together and learn team work by training in cooperation.

An interesting feature of university centres for health sciences is their organization into the basic or fundamental aspects of all health sciences education: biomedical laboratory sciences; hospital clinical sciences; and public-health sciences.

Different members of the health team require different proportions of these basic ingredients, but they all require all three. These basic divisions are represented by appropriate physical structures (buildings and equipment) and are staffed by personnel (academic, technical or administrative) in the appropriate disciplines.

Teaching methodology in health sciences education

Effective use of available funds for total health care - delivering an optimum package to each family, community or population group - presupposes the availability of personnel trained to work as a team (to minimize waste and promote effectiveness) *and* an efficient health service organization. Team training should therefore be the goal, even in traditionally organized institutions. The stages in planning the work of the team are as follows:

1. Making an assessment of the basic needs of the district or country.
2. Deciding what 'globally' is the work required on the services that must be rendered to satisfy these basic needs.
3. Next, dividing the 'global task' among a number of health professionals and auxiliaries.
4. Defining the tasks of each of these health personnel, ensuring at the same time a certain specificity (or 'specialization') as well as 'polyvalence'.

After defining the tasks for each member of the team, educational objectives are then defined with the aim of ensuring that the student, at the end of his training, is capable of undertaking these tasks competently. Hence there will be educational objectives for medical, nursing, technical and other personnel. These broad objectives are termed *institutional*; each division (biomedical sciences, public health, hospital, clinical) defines more detailed *divisional* objectives. Schools with departments prepare *departmental* objectives. Finally individual teachers will define their *specific* instructional objectives. The actual teaching programme and the evaluation is based on the objectives so defined. It is very important that these objectives be realistic; they should seek to give the student a suitable orientation and, for those working in African child-health care, a full awareness of the dilemma of quality, quantity and cost.

Educational programmes should be designed in such a manner that multiprofessional teaching and team training can be practised as much as possible: here is the advantage of integrated teaching based on 'themes' or 'activities' as opposed to traditional departmental teaching. A professor of nutrition who organized different courses for medical students, nurses, technical staff and health inspectors and for specialist nutrition, dietetics and biochemistry students must have a very large department with a large staff and spacious teaching facilities. On the other hand, where human nutrition is a part of integrated teaching programmes and constitutes a theme, albeit a very important theme, students of different health professions can share in a few core programmes. Some will need to take the whole course, ranging from the simplest to the most complex aspects, others will drop off the course at points appropriate to their previously defined educational objectives. Even more important, practical field assignments can be easily shared by different categories of students of the health professions; each category performs functions corresponding to the tasks they will eventually be called upon to accomplish at the end of their training.

Similar remarks will apply to major biomedical sciences (like physiology, pathology, anatomy, microbiology), public-health sciences (epidemiology, biostatistics, nutrition, applied parasitology/entomology, medical sociology, social psychology, health administration, etc.) and major clinical disciplines (medicine, surgery, paediatrics, obstetrics, psychiatry, etc.). Integrated teaching e.g. by organic systems allows for planned symposia or themes, with the participation of teachers of different disciplines in biomedical sciences, clinical medicine or public health. In order to ensure the quality or academic level, only students with comparable academic entry qualifications will share certain symposia, e.g. medical, dental or pharmacy students who have full university entry qualifications. Nursing, technical and social-welfare students will also share certain theoretical courses or symposia. But, as stated already, all students whatever their previous academic attainments can work together in health teams - in hospital wards and outpatient clinics, in the context of family health or family medicine within a defined community, and in the delivery of total health care to the population groups in peripheral/rural communities. It must be emphasized to all students that health education and health services organization are indispensable components of the core-curricula.

It is recommended that evaluation of students be as objective as possible; it should test the knowledge, skills and attitudes (if possible) stated in the previously defined educational objectives. Assessment should be by periodic class tests, e.g. after each 'system' or 'theme' studied, and by end-of-year examinations. In the periodic class tests students would be expected to present as much detail as is desired (within the framework of their future roles); but in final end-of-year examinations they must demonstrate that they have integrated all they have learnt, that they understand the broad principles, have cultivated the appropriate attitudes and possess the most important skills. Promotion to the next class will depend upon the summation of the results of the class tests and the end-of-year examination. The results of all examinations should be a feedback to both teachers and students.

Specific training in African child-health care
Is there a need to train practitioners or health teams to focus on African child-health problems? The demographic pattern in African countries, in which as much as 50 per cent of the population may be under the age of 20 years, suggests a positive answer. A case could be made out for training paediatric practitioners: medical, nursing and so on. They could have an abbreviated basic medical or nursing education followed by early specialization. The argument against is in

The mothers will come if they think it's worth while

fact that infections and parasitic disease on the one hand, and malnutrition on the other, are the major problems, and one might therefore argue that what is needed is a greater emphasis on preventive medicine. If the paediatrics problem is acute, and urgent, it is mainly because of the vulnerability of the young child. There is also the necessity not to separate child care from maternal care.

A good case can be made for the training of large numbers of nurse-specialists, highly skilled in maternal and child care. It is on such a group that must fall the major burden and responsibility. They will seek advice from paediatricians, obstetricians and primary-care physicians (general practitioners of medicine), and in peripheral centres (where most of the work is maternal and child care) these MCH nurse-specialists could be the leaders of the local health team. They could also collaborate in appropriate circumstances with social-welfare and other workers in preparing parents for parenthood; with paediatricians, obstetricians, nutritionists and preventive-medicine specialists in perinatal care, infant nutrition and vaccination programmes; and with social-welfare workers, environmental hygienists, laboratory technicians and medical psychologists, etc., in family welfare and child-spacing, hygiene and environmental sanitation and the socialization process (as previously defined). One would therefore see the role of the nurse-practitioner-specialist in mother-and-child care as vital in the effort to achieve an optimum-package solution to the quality/quantity/cost problem facing health administrators in Africa today.

Lessons from the Developing Countries

Derrick B. Jelliffe and E.F. Patrice Jelliffe

The countries that are less-developed economically are also, through lack of resources, less dependent upon western medical technology, some aspects of which are coming to be seen as increasingly harmful and counterproductive. The authors consider a number of traditional third-world techniques and childbirth practices that may now seem biologically, socially and economically more fruitful than western equivalents.

Ideas, philosophies and techniques have always travelled from one part of the world to another. During recent decades, with the development of rapid air transport and electronic communications, this process has increased dramatically in intensity and speed, with a particularly massive extension of technology in recent decades from the industrialized countries of North America and Europe to so-called less-developed parts of the world.

The overriding importance of scientific technology in health services has been a universal assumption for modern medical planners, and the same emphases have been often rather uncritically and even somewhat arrogantly exported to different cultures and circumstances in developing countries, particularly during colonial times, but also sometimes in the course of international assistance programmes.

In fact, there seems increasing evidence that technology has been overemphasized in western countries [16]. Economical application for the majority has not been given sufficient emphasis, nor have biological aspects of health care.

As part of this realization, it is apparent that developing countries have lessons to give to the world from their current systems of child care, and these may be considered in two categories: the *traditional and biological* and the *adaptive-technology* lessons.

Traditional and biological lessons

An infinite variety of different customs and practices exist in the many different cultures in developing countries, including, as anywhere, many harmful practices. However, in general, many traditional methods appear to be more biologically sound in relation to childbirth, to the care of the extero-gestate foetus (birth to 9 months) and 'transitional' *[5]*, and to harmonious interrelationships between mother and child.

Childbirth and the newborn. It is becoming appreciated by many observers that the management of childbirth in the western world is related, correctly, to the prevention of sepsis and avoidance of obstetrical complications ('navigation of the birth-canal'), while, at the same time, the methods used seem to lay undue emphasis on regimentation of mothers and babies, and on the convenience of the medical, nursing and administrative staff.

Western obstetrical practice has been called 'the cultural warping of childbirth' *[3]* and, without undue prejudice, very many aspects of more orthodox obstetrics in Europe and North America do seem strangely unbiological, for example, inadequate emotional preparation for labour, the routine use of anaesthesia and episiotomies, the early clamping of the umbilical cord, the unnecessary shaving of the pubic hair, the position during labour and the extraordinary practice of separating the newborn from the mother. It seems increasingly probable that not only are most of these practices undesirable or routinely unnecessary, but that they have physical and psychological ill-effects on both mother and newborn *[3]*.

By contrast, traditional practices during childbirth in many parts of the world, including Africa, appear to be biologically much more sound, although often with greater hazards bacteriologically and from the point of view of obstetrical mechanics.

In particular, traditional practices are often based on what Raphael has called the *doula* concept *[14]*. Studies in social mammals and in many traditional cultures by this investigator indicated that a constant feature during the end of pregnancy, labour and the early weeks of neonatal life was one or more individuals, usually a female, who had a *doula* function. That is to say, a female assistant who gave physical and emotional assistance and also acted as supplier of information based on local tradition and experience *[14]*. The result was a confident, informed mother with physical and psychological support immediately available. This tended to minimize the fears and doubts that can so easily occur at this time of stress and, in particular, supplied the necessary atmosphere of certainty so important in the initiation of lactation.

The contrast in western cultures is very great indeed. No longer is the community completely supportive of breast-feeding and, even for the mother who refuses to breast-feed her baby, the psychosocial situation of the average obstetrical hospital in the western world is almost anti-*doula* in effect. However, it must be noted that, largely as a result of the gradual pressures of increasing numbers of women's groups this is gradually being changed.

It would be most unfortunate if the psychologically well-tried and supportive methods found in many traditional cultures in Africa should be displaced by the antiseptic, regimented approaches found in orthodox obstetrics in the western world until recently. This is, indeed, a major area from which the western world can learn from traditional societies in developing countries *[6, 14]*.

Child-bearing and socialization. The psychological and emotional adjustment of children to the local cultures and needs seems much more likely to be developed smoothly and appropriately if the methods used in traditional societies are followed rather than the learning at school 'by the book, about the book, for the book' with little relevance to preparation for living [7].

In later childhood, the traditional methods of play, rearing and socialization in general in African cultures help to prepare the young boy and girl for their appropriate roles in the future in the actual circumstances of the particular community [7].

Young-child nutrition. Knowledge of nutrients was not available in traditional cultures in any part of the world, although many communities recognized the social significance of various forms of malnutrition. Thus, in several African languages, a word was used for the severe form of protein-energy malnutrition now known in international medical terminology as kwashiorkor. For example, in Uganda, a word of similar meaning, *obwosi*, was used, also implying a condition occurring in the 'displaced' child. Words with this type of meaning clearly indicated that the significance of the displacement of the young child from the breast milk by the arrival of another pregnancy or sibling was a recognized precursor in this form of malnutrition.

The main lesson to be learned from developing countries is in relation to breast-feeding. At least in rural areas in non-industrialized countries, breast-feeding is still, for the most part, easy, uneventful and represents an immense benefit from the nutritional and anti-infective point of view, particularly in relation to the prophylaxis of diarrhoeal disease [8]. Indeed, it is extremely difficult to conceive of anything else which could have the cost-effectiveness of breast-feeding and human milk, and overcome the distribution and logistic problems (so often commented on) of 'reaching the infant and pre-school child' [10].

Mother's milk: still the best

In past and present-day traditional societies, including those in Africa, it is well recognized that the transitional or weaning period is the one of greatest nutritional stress, with the exception of the urbanized poor, for whom the earlier onset of protein-energy malnutrition, in the form of marasmus, is resulting increasingly from shortening periods of lactation [5].

In other words, the 'danger period' is particularly during the second year of life, when the child is actively in the process of transition from a diet solely of mother's milk to a complete adjustment to the local ecological problems, including bacterial and parasitic infections, a share of the full adult diet, etc.

In the past when there was less contact with the outside world, there may well have been various factors responsible for a better nutritional transition from extero-gestate foetus to older childhood. First, there is the child-spacing effect of successful, uncomplemented lactation [9]. This undoubtedly has considerable importance as far as nutrition is concerned. Second, in many communities there may have been the use of a wider range of food than currently available. For example, in Uganda in the early years of the present century it seems likely that much more high-protein sesame was used in general and also in the preparation of weaning foods. Likewise, with the increasing deviation towards urbanization or at least an urban life style, there has been a tendency towards the decreasing use of a variety of semi-wild foods, particularly dark-green leafy vegetables.

Child-spacing. Child-spacing has been achieved principally by the endocrinological and biological effect of prolonged lactation, unsupplemented in the early months with other foods [9]. Recent hormonal investigations have clearly shown that this is the direct measurable consequence of increased secretion of prolactin produced by suckling at the breast. It has also been shown that this remarkable hormone, prolactin, not only is responsible for the secretion of milk in the breast, but also has the important additional effects of inhibiting ovulation, decreasing urine secretion (thereby deviating body water needed for the synthesis of human milk) and a psycho-cerebral effect which can be termed an increase in 'motherliness' [11].

The child-spacing effect of lactation has been difficult for some people to appreciate, perhaps understandably, because of the pregnancies that can be observed in women who are still breast-feeding. It is important to realize that the anti-ovulation effect of prolactin is related to the *amount* of this hormone which is produced, which in turn is proportional to the amount of suckling at the breast [9]. If other foods in the form of artificial feeds or solids are introduced in the early weeks of life, then the amount of prolactin will be decreased. In any case, as the young child grows and other foods are introduced so the amount of suckling will be diminished and the contraceptive effect of prolactin wear off [9].

It is not surprising that such a process exists in man. It is, in fact, a parallel with the hormone-dictated 'mating season' in other mammals. Without such a spacing device, it is doubtful if man could have survived. In addition, in many traditional communities, including some of those in Africa, the period between births was also increased by a variety of different customs and practices [6], which were aimed at preventing the too early resumption of sexual intercourse. Thus, in some societies, the mother would stay apart from the husband until the child could walk or talk or had a culturally defined number of teeth, etc.

Adaptive-technology lessons

In the so-called western world, recent medical developments stem largely from the dramatic and, indeed, revolutionary scientific advances that have emerged from the middle of the nineteenth century until the present time. These include bacteriology, dating back to Pasteur; aseptic and antiseptic surgery, introduced by Lister; X-rays, discovered by Röntgen, etc. While these spectacular discoveries did indeed revolutionize modern medicine, it may well be that they may have tended to overemphasize curative and technological aspects of the subject, with hospitals as the pinnacle of this whole process.

In past centuries in Europe, hospitals were largely collecting places for the indigent, the dying and those with severe and unacceptable infectious diseases. After the scientific medical revolution, the hospital changed to the main centre for technological medicine, and everything became geared to these ends, as for example, the operating theatre for surgery and the radiological departments for X-ray investigations. Within these new technology-dominated hospitals, the medical and nursing staff were firmly in control, as a quasi-military organization, even with well-marked uniforms indicating different levels of status and of authority. Patients under these circumstances tended to be handled firmly and paternalistically from a standpoint of technological superiority, while little concern was shown for their biological and emotional needs, which were little understood, particularly those of children. In turn, the whole system was perpetuated by the training of health staff geared to such hospital-based technology.

In Africa during colonial times a similar pattern was imported and, indeed, it may be argued that one of the least valuable aspects of colonial domination may well have been the inappropriate form of training of physicians and nurses, and some aspects of the health service which were introduced then and which are still dominant.

However, because of the very scale of the problems, and because of very limited resources of staff, money, education and equipment ('the shortage syndrome'), many adaptive changes were made within such systems, often without it being formally recognized by the establishment that such changes were, in fact, occurring, or without necessarily having full approval for them.

Again, until the last few years in recently independent countries, such developments, based on the application of 'intermediate technology' and the use of auxiliaries, were rather resentfully regarded as 'mud-hut medicine'. The situation has now changed considerably and, perhaps rather ironically, such developments which have been widespread in developing countries for decades, are now much debated and experimented with in industrialized countries as advanced and *avant-garde.* Some of these aspects may be considered here.

Children's wards. In so-called developed countries, it has become recognized in recent decades that the practice of abandoning the frightened, sick young child to the psychological and physical traumas of the hospital is to be avoided or curtailed as far as possible. In this regard, many hospitals in parts of Africa are vastly in advance of those in

Europe and North America [2]. In most places, it is fortunately still the practice for mothers to come in with their young children whenever possible.

Plainly, this has disadvantages, notably in the disorganization of ward routine, problems of cleanliness, the provision of food, the need for toilet and sleeping arrangements for the mothers, possible interference with treatment, and so on. At the same time, the advantages of such systems vastly outweigh these disadvantages. The mother is present to comfort and reassure the child in this very strange environment, to act as a highly sensitive 'human electronic monitoring apparatus', to assist with feeding the child and some aspects of his care and treatment and, in particular, to be available for nutrition and health education in and around the ward. It is especially this last function that should make the practice so very worth while and, what is more, it is this function that may convert the traditional clinical bastion of the hospital into what it should be - an amalgam of clinical and preventive work.

Maternity wards. The maternity wards imported into Africa and other developing countries from the western world are based on procedures that can be regarded more and more as a 'cultural warping of childbirth' [3]. We have already noted, that the traditional practices are very often less effective bacteriologically and from the point of view of obstetrical mechanics. At the same time, they are usually infinitely superior for the psycho-biological support of the mother during this difficult period and for the successful initiation to breast-feeding.

Auxiliaries and staff duties. For very many years, in various parts of Africa, a wide variety of different auxiliaries and other less classical cadres have been used very successfully. For example, in Francophone West Africa, before the Second World War, staff with very little background education or literacy were used effectively in large-scale anti-trypanosomiasis campaigns. Likewise, in severe outbreaks of cerebrospinal fever that occurred in the southern Sudan in the 1940s, a variety of auxiliaries were used very effectively to detect cases and treat with twice-daily intramuscular injections of sulphapyridine. Very effective training has also been carried out for many decades in the Sudan with indigenous midwives in the school of Omdurman.

Compressed management. In African and other developing countries, because of limited staff and difficulties in contacting people owing to distance or poor transport, various forms of what may be termed 'compressed management' have been devised. For example, attempts have been made to try to use immunization procedures for young children that entail using as many vaccines as possible at one time, with fewer attendances. Similarly, many varieties of 'monodosage' have been employed or suggested [15]. In these, various drugs or other pharmaceuticals are given by intramuscular depot injection or by mouth for slow absorption and effectiveness over a period of some time.

Conclusions

It cannot be contended that in the past rural Africa represented a uniformly joyful Arcadia of contented, healthy children, and it cannot be denied, moreover, that modern technological science has been a major factor in the improvement of health, including that of young children. Yet it seems increasingly clear that what is required is a balance between 'technomania' and a 'romantic regression to the past'

[16]. In the western world, unbalanced scientific technology seems in some ways to have gone too far, and a reaction against this has developed that manifests itself, for example, in the trend towards breast-feeding and an emphasis on more traditional 'natural' foods and in an interest in less technologically dominated systems - in the methods of preparation for childbirth without anaesthesia, for example. Science and technology need to be blended with methods, characteristic of African cultures, that are psychologically and emotionally reassuring, more 'biological' and better adapted to human requirement. The flow of information and inspiration should be two-way.

REFERENCES
1. American Public Health Association. *Development and Evaluation of Integrated Delivery Systems (DEIDS).* 1972.
2. Bell, J.E. *The Family in Hospital: Lessons from Developing Countries.* Washington DC, US Government Printing Office, 1969.
3. Haire, D. *The Cultural Warping of Childbirth.* Milwaukee, Wis., International Childbirth Education Association, 1972.
4. International Union of Nutritional Sciences. Report of Committee II.3. The Zagreb Guidelines. *Nutr.Abstr.,* January 1973.
5. Jelliffe, D.B. The Pre-School Child as a Bio-Cultural Transitional. *J.Trop.Pediat.,* Vol.14: 217, 1968.
6. Jelliffe, D.B.; Bennett, F.J. World-wide Care of Mothers and Newborn. *Clin.Obst.Gynec.,* Vol.5: 64, 1972.
7. ——; ——. Aspects of Child Rearing in Africa. *J.Trop.Pediat.Envir.Child Hlth,* Vol.18: 25, 1972.
8. Jelliffe, D.B.; Jelliffe, E.F.P. The Uniqueness of Human Milk. *Am.J.Clin.Nutr.,* Vol.24: 968, 1971.
9. ——; ——. Lactation, Conception and the Nutrition of the Nursing Mother and Child. *J.Pediat.,* Vol.81: 829, 1972.
10. ——; ——. Education for Lactation: Public Health Program. *Ecol.Fd.Nutr.* 1973.
11. ——; ——. *The Physiological and Economic Significance of Human Milk in Modern World Ecology.* 1973.
12. Morley, D. A Health Service for the Under Fives. *Trans.Roy.Soc.Trop.Med.Hyg.,* Vol.57: 79, 1963.
13. Neumann, A.K.; Prince, J.; Gilbert, F.; Lourie, I.M. The Danfa/Ghana Rural Health and Family Planning Project. *Ghana Med.J.,* Vol.2: 18, 1972.
14. Raphael, D. The Lactation-Suckling Process within a Matrix of Supportive Behavior. New York, NY, Columbia University, 1966. (PhD thesis.)
15. Stanfield, J.P.; Jelliffe, D.B. Monodosage - A Practical Compromise in Tropical Countries. *J.Trop.Pediat.,* Vol.13: 152, 1967.
16. Taylor, G.T. *Re-Think: A Paraprimitive Solution.* New York, NY, Dutton, 1973.
17. Taylor, H.C.; Berelson, B. Comprehensive Family Planning Based on Maternal/Child Health Services: A Feasibility Study for a World Program. *Stud. Family Plann.,* Vol.2: 22, 1971.
18. Williams, C.D. Maternal and Child Health in Kumasi in 1935. *J.Trop.Pediat.,* Vol.3: 141, 1956.
19. Williams, C.D.; Jelliffe, D.B. *Mother and Child Health: Delivering the Services.* London, Oxford University Press, 1972.

The Chinese Experience

The organizers of the Addis Ababa seminar were privileged to receive, as guest lecturers, two distinguished medical experts from the People's Republic of China, Dr Lin Chuan-chia, head of the Child Health Care Department of the Peking Children's Hospital, and Dr Li Pao-ai, head of the Paediatric Department at the Teaching Hospital, Tientsin Medical College. Both doctors stayed throughout the duration of the seminar, taking an active part in its proceedings, and also kindly answered questions on medical care in China. The seminar participants were particularly interested in putting questions on child care and the answers to some of these questions are printed here.

Some Questions Answered

By Dr Lin Chuan-chia
and Dr Li Pao-ai

What is the infant mortality situation in China?

The 1972 infant mortality rate in Shanghai of 8.7 mentioned in our report[*] is the rate in urban Shanghai per 1,000 live births under 1 year old. This is to be compared with the infant mortality rate of 150 per 1,000 in 1948 in Shanghai proper. Such a rate is not common, however, in China, for the development of woman and child care in different regions is not even. Generally speaking, the infant mortality in many districts is higher than that of Shanghai.

The following steps were taken to reduce infant mortality:

1. Health centres for women and children were set up. Since the founding of the People's Republic of China in 1949, the concern of our party and government is shown in the attention paid to the health of women and children. Health centres, manned by professional and spare-time medical

[*] *Child Health Care in New China,* Peking, Chinese Medical Association, 1 May 1973.

workers, have been established by central, provincial, municipal and county public-health institutions. There are maternity and children's hospitals or clinics in cities. In general hospitals above county level and hospitals for workers and staff of enterprises, there are usually departments of obstetrics and gynaecology, and of paediatrics. In the countryside, there are clinics in people's communes, and production brigades have midwives and women 'barefoot doctors'. All these institutions have constituted an initial network of health protection for women and children in both urban and rural areas.

2. The principle of 'prevention first' is put into practice. In many districts, common diseases of women are examined and treated. Medical workers not only examine and treat women patients but also disseminate knowledge about disease prevention and the protection of women labour, and take measures to prevent common diseases.

3. Measures are taken to protect the health of pregnant women. Women workers and commune members are given lighter jobs after pregnancy and are freed from night shifts from the seventh month of pregnancy. The physical condition of the foetus has been improved by taking these measures. For instance, the average weight of 854 newborn infants delivered in Peking Maternity Hospital in 1971 was 3.253 kg, while that of 658 newborn infants delivered in the same hospital in 1952 was 3.116 kg.

4. Scientific delivery methods are popularized. In cities hospital delivery is universal. In the countryside, midwives and women 'barefoot doctors' have been trained in asepsis and the incidence of neonatal tetanus has thus been considerably reduced.

5. Breast-feeding is encouraged. Lactating women workers are not assigned to night shifts and to nurse their babies they can have a one-hour period off during working hours every day for one year after parturition. In the countryside, lactating mothers are assigned to work in fields near their houses. Medical workers propagate the advantages of breast-feeding, introduce weaning methods and give directions on scientific child-rearing and timely increases of supplementary food and nutrients such as cod-liver oil and vitamin D.

6. A variety of vaccines are administered for the control of infectious diseases.

What is the situation with regard to family planning?

Since the People's Republic was founded, women, enjoying equal political and economic rights with men, have taken an active part in social work and productive labour. The desire to work energetically for the construction of socialism has prompted them to practise family planning. Moreover, planned increase in population is our established policy. We apply such a policy not because we face the problem of 'overpopulation'. It is true that the population in China has grown rather quickly after liberation, but production has increased at an even greater rate. In the twenty-four years to 1973, China's population grew from more than 500 million to over 700 million, a rate of 50 per cent, but during the same period, grain output increased from 110 million tons to 240 million tons, a rate of more than 200 per cent.

In order to complete the emancipation of women, to improve the people's health, to rear a wholesome younger generation and to bring about national prosperity, population increase has to be kept in check. Late marriage and the practice of birth control are essential measures to this end. Under the guidance of medical workers, married couples undertake contraception appropriate to their age and physical condition. Public-health institutions at all levels and social organizations encourage the married through extensive propaganda and education to practise birth control voluntarily. The state supplies contraceptives free of charge and medical workers even deliver contraceptives to those who need them.

What training do 'barefoot doctors' receive?

'Barefoot doctors' are commune members who have had some basic medical training and give treatment without leaving farm work. They get the name because in southern China peasants work barefooted in paddy fields.

Since the cultural revolution, more than 1 million 'barefoot doctors' have been fostered, of whom over 300,000 are women. Generally speaking, every countryside production brigade has about three 'barefoot doctors', including one woman, trained in the following way. Promising young people selected and recommended by production brigades are brought together for a short-term training course conducted by doctors from county hospitals, clinics of people's communes or mobile medical teams. They learn general knowledge on internal medicine, surgery, paediatrics, Chinese traditional medicine, Chinese herb medicine and acupuncture. The teachers adhere to the principle of integrating theory with practice and of combining class lectures with clinical study in teaching. Trainees usually receive eighteen months of training, spread over three years during the farming slack seasons. After completing their training, some are assigned to work for a certain period in clinics of people's communes, county hospitals or general hospitals in cities. By taking part in practice they acquire more medical knowledge and gain experience in diagnosis and treatment.

The main duties of barefoot doctors' are: (a) to disseminate knowledge on hygiene, as well as on the prevention and treatment of diseases, and to urge the masses to take due measures; (b) to organize health and sanitation campaigns to improve environmental hygiene by exterminating pests and by obtaining suitable control of sewage and to ensure the cleanliness of food and drinking water; (c) to give BCG and DPT inoculations and vaccines against polio, smallpox and measles to children under 7; (d) to treat common and recurrent illnesses, dress wounds and give first aid; (e) to cultivate and collect medical herbs and compound them into medicine; (f) to glean information on the incidence of infectious diseases and to instruct the masses to take measures such as segregation and sterilization.

'Barefoot doctors' have played a considerable role in medical and health work in the rural areas and they are popular among the masses. But our experience in training them is far from complete. We have to tackle, for example, the problem of raising their medical skill more rapidly. Only by solving this problem can their ranks be expanded and the role played by them be enlarged.

The Early Years of Childhood

The Drama of Infant Growth

Bo Vahlquist

Extra concentration on the child is justified in the light of the child's special vulnerability. Professor Vahlquist describes the immense evolutionary journey that has to be made by every human embryo even before childhood proper has begun - and the growing certainty that an unfavourable early environment may lead to lasting injury.

Introduction

Let us start with the question: why is it that the early years are so important, even crucial for the individual, irrespective of whether we consider the short-range or the long-range prospect?

Let us first consider for a moment the period *before* birth. Within the lapse of a few months following conception, each foetus has to pass at great speed through a long series of transitions which reflect the evolution of the animal kingdom over billions of years. It then proceeds to stages of growth and development in which it makes enormous headway both *in utero* and then during the first few years of extra-uterine life. It is only to be expected that a human being will be extremely vulnerable during these periods of intense transitions, growth and development.

Another obvious reason why the early years are so important is that during this period of life the human being is completely dependent on its environment for support and protection. Left to itself, it will succumb almost instantaneously.

For these reasons - its great vulnerability and its complete dependence on external help - every child born represents a great challenge both to the family and to the community to take the responsibility of providing it with its minimal needs. Every child which dies or survives with handicaps due to defects in the environment represents a failure which should not be taken lightly.

Normal growth and development

Body weight and height are still the best and at the same time the simplest indicators of whether a child is thriving or not. Growth charts, giving the normal mean and range for

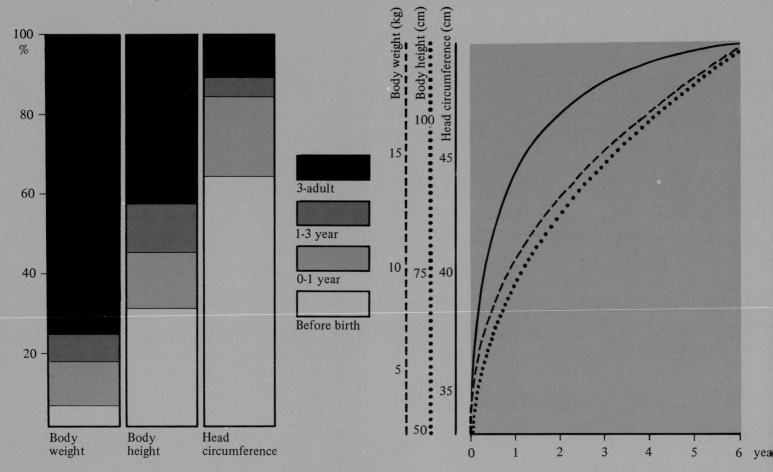

The drama of infant growth

100 %
80
60
40
20

Body weight
Body height
Head circumference

3-adult

1-3 year

0-1 year

Before birth

Body weight (kg)
Body height (cm)
Head circumference (cm)

15

10

5

100

75

50

45

40

35

0   1   2   3   4   5   6   year

increase in weight and height with age, have long been used at well-baby clinics in the technically developed world and they are gradually being introduced also in the developing countries. There is no better way of revealing at an early stage impending disturbances to the well-being of the child than to draw up its weight curve.

It is worth remembering that in the short span of one year after its birth the child's body weight will normally increase by more than 200 per cent and its height by 50 per cent. Obviously, the child's demands on the quality and the quantity of its food intake per unit of body weight will be very great. Even after the first year the growth speed remains very high for quite some time. Along with these changes in the pattern of growth, far-reaching changes in biochemical composition and enzyme activities also take place. For example, the water content of the body, which at birth is 75 per cent, at the age of 1 year is only 59 per cent. The high water content of the body, coupled with the still immature function of the kidneys, makes the young child very sensitive to dehydration, a fact recognized by all paediatricians but not always by laymen.

Likewise, the first few years mean gross changes in the fat and protein contents of the body, which change from 11 per cent to 24 per cent and from 11 per cent to 15 per cent at birth and at the age of 1 year, respectively. For water and fat most of these changes take place as early as the first two months of life [8]. For the enzymes typical age-related 'growth patterns' can also be outlined.

The critical periods of development
It is only during the last decade that we have learned that growth itself changes fundamentally in character during various stages of the life of the young. We can now make a distinction between a period when the tissues grow through the multiplication of cells (*hyperplasia*) and a period when they grow through increases in the sizes of individual cells (*hypertrophy*). In between the two, there is a transitional period when both hyperplasia and hypertrophy exist side by side. The transition from one type of growth to the other occurs at different times in different organs, even at different times in different parts of one and the same organ.

Now let us consider this fundamentally important new knowledge. If the process of multiplication of cells is not completed at the normal moment in time, then there is no possibility of catching up later. Hence the organs or part of organs involved will remain suboptimal for life with respect to the total number of functioning cells.

In the development of different organs, like the liver, the kidneys or the brain, there are periods when growth due to cell multiplication occurs at increased speed (the term 'growth spurt' has been used). During these periods, the organs are more sensitive than at other times to unfavourable influences from the environment. For this reason, they have been termed 'critical periods' [3]. Just as the body as a whole exhibits a growth spurt in the pre- and early postnatal period, so do several individual organs, among them the brain. This is true of man and of several other species, at any rate. The effect of malnutrition will be especially far-reaching if it is present at this time.

The 'anatomy' of the unfavourable environment
A host of factors can be incriminated that act, usually synergistically, to the disadvantage of the child: poverty, poor lodging, primitive hygiene, disease-provoking germs, inadequate

access to medical aid, ignorance and, last but not least, under-and malnutrition. All these factors contribute to a high sickness rate and an excessive loss of life, even before productive age.

As far as physical health is concerned, the two most relevant and immediate causes of concern are malnutrition and infections/parasitoses. There is a synergism between the two. Everyday experience teaches us that infectious diseases, especially if they involve fever or are accompanied by diarrhoea, may compromise the nutritional status. More recent is the recognition that this is true also the other way round, i.e. that malnutrition may increase the susceptibility to infectious diseases and worsen their course. In other words, a real vicious circle exists here [14].

An often-quoted observation in this respect relates to measles. In industrial countries, this is an unpleasant but harmless disease. In many developing countries, it is a highly dangerous disease, with fatality figures of up to 5 per cent or more at times. There is no difference in the germs, but there is a difference in the hosts, represented by populations of generally malnourished children.

The conclusion from a practical standpoint of all this is that malnutrition and its evil effects can best be fought by a combination of programmes that aim at an improved intake of food as well as at the prevention of infections/parasitoses.

The interplay between genetic endowment and environment
The genes are capable of delivering their message, whether it is ultimately concerned with body stature, brain growth or the colour of the eyes, in a singular and predetermined way, even under greatly differing conditions in the environment. However, under certain given conditions, with gross distortion of the environment, the given predetermined goal may never be reached. In extreme cases the effect may be lethal but in less extreme cases the effect of the environment may be compatible with life and yet conspicuous. It is in this latter case that we are confronted with a situation where the effect of the early unfavourable influence of the environment truly has a lifelong effect in that the adult never corresponds to his genetic endowment.

It was only some thirty years ago that the possibility of environmental influence causing malformations in human beings was widely recognized through observations of the effect of rubella on the young foetus [9] and it was less than twenty years ago that the possibility of environmental influences causing permanent subnormality in the physical development of human beings was first hinted at [10]. Only now are we in the process of reaching a balanced conclusion as to the effect of early malnutrition on mental development. It is obvious, then, that problems of fundamental importance, not only for individuals but indirectly for whole nations, and especially so for developing countries, are only now being clarified and correctly evaluated.

The long-term sequelae of an early unfavourable environment
When long-term sequelae of an early unfavourable environment were discussed in earlier days, it was in relation to chronically diseased organs and locally manifest specific handicaps of various kinds. A complicated delivery with intracranial haemorrhage or with severe asphyxia could leave the child permanently disabled, with the clinical picture of cerebral palsy. A liver disease could lead up to chronic

dysfunction through liver cirrhosis. A traffic accident and subsequent amputation of a limb could leave the child permanently crippled.

During the last decade, the matter of the long-term sequelae has acquired a new dimension, which widens the concept considerably. It is now recognized that the sequelae may be of a much more subtle character than the examples just referred to and yet constitute a clear-cut handicap in the life of the individual. What I am referring to is the fundamentally important observation that an unfavourable environment at an early period of life, and particularly protein-energy malnutrition (PEM) in conjunction with infections, can permanently interfere with normal growth and development.

Early malnutrition, brain growth and mental development
Traditionally, the brain has been held to be very resistant to undernutrition, even if this is severe in character. As an example may be mentioned studies on pigs, in which severe undernutrition had caused body weight to remain at only 3.5 per cent of the normal at 1 year of age, whereas the brain weight was 66 per cent of the normal [13]. There was none the less a reduction in the weight of the brain and the undernourished animals also showed various signs indicating disturbance of the central nervous function.

Severe PEM - admittedly usually combined with other distortion of the environment - will also cause retardation of brain growth in human beings. This has been demonstrated both *in vivo* by measuring head circumference and at autopsy by measuring brain weight. With new techniques it is possible to analyse the situation somewhat more in depth. A series of studies of this kind have been carried out in cooperation between the Department of Paediatrics, Uppsala, and the Ethiopian Nutrition Institute, Addis Ababa. They show that in severe PEM - and particularly in the acute stage of kwashiorkor - pronounced changes may occur with respect to brain size [4,5,6] and, incidentally, also with respect to function of the peripheric nerves [7].

We have discussed the effects of an unfavourable early environment, malnutrition in particular, on the growth and development of the brain. What do we know about the effect on mental function? To what extent can poverty in its widest sense so influence the young child that it produces a lasting subnormality with respect to mental function? In a review published in the *WHO Chronicle* [11] discussing the outcome of a recent symposium on early malnutrition and mental development [2] the following cautious conclusions were drawn:'. . . in spite of the widely held and widely publicized opinion that malnutrition in early life jeopardizes mental development, the evidence to support this opinion - especially that from studies conducted in man - is scanty. Furthermore, most of the work has been carried out on children suffering from extreme degrees of malnutrition and there is practically no evidence of a relationship between the much commoner mild and moderate forms of malnutrition and mental retardation. What seems probable is that there is an interaction between malnutrition and other environmental factors, especially social stimulation, and that the child's ultimate intellectual status is the resultant of this interaction.'

The importance of the early years
in the industrial society

Relatively speaking, the risks are also high for young
children in industrial society. However, for a country like
Sweden, the defects in the environment which influence
the child in an unfavourable way are strikingly different in
character from those of a developing country. With respect
to nutrition they are linked with excess rather than with
deficiency. Overeating and overnutrition with calories are
being discussed, particularly since the early years may be
decisive also in this respect and may lay the foundation of
obesity later in life. Further, the effects of the
overconsumption of fat, especially of saturated fatty acids,
have caused considerable apprehension in recent years. I
shall dwell on this problem for a moment.

The level of cholesterol in the blood has for a good many
years attracted special attention, since there is evidence of
a connexion between a high cholesterol level and the
tendency to develop atherosclerosis. The Ethiopian
Nutrition Institute studied the situation in different areas
of Ethiopia and found significantly lower levels of
cholesterol in non-privileged Ethiopian children compared
with privileged Ethiopian children, who themselves revealed
somewhat lower levels than in privileged Swedish children
[1]. There is reason to believe that in this case the
comparatively low values in non-privileged children
probably have their origin in a low dietary fat intake. From
the point of view of atherosclerosis in adult and old age,
the non-privileged Ethiopian children should be in a *better*
situation than the privileged children in Addis Ababa or in
Sweden. The advantage of a low value of cholesterol in the
blood is not unlimited, however. In the Ethiopian province
of Sidamo, we have seen values that are so low for both
the dietary intake of fat and the mean cholesterol levels that
the possibility of a true fat deficiency must be considered.

Adaptability to the environment

Over the millennia more or less all the species on the earth
have had to adapt themselves to changing ecologies. The
transition from life in the water to life on land is one
example.

It is of great theoretical and practical importance to know to
what extent such adaptive processes are making themselves
apparent also between groups of human beings living today
but under very different conditions in different parts of the
world. Before considering this, we must realize that in the
life of mankind it is only for a very short space of time that
some groups of human beings, living in what we usually call
the industrialized countries, have raised themselves above the
threat of recurring malnutrition and uncontrollable severe
infections to an existence of reasonable affluence and
stability.

We have to make a distinction between healthy and
unhealthy adaptation. If a majority of children in the
developing countries are retarded and maybe definitely
stunted in growth, this is an unhealthy adaptation. Growth
needs (in terms of protein - energy requirement, etc.) may
be reduced but so also is the fitness of the subject. Examples
that can be mentioned are in the reduced resistance to
infectious diseases and reduced physical working capacity.

Large population groups on this earth, both children and
adults, have a dietary intake of calories, protein and other
nutrients that rarely comes anywhere near the recommended
allowances and still the majority of them survive and still

they function, at least within limits. Two reasons may be given in explanation. First, the recommended allowances in the western world are often 'generous' and have a considerable safety margin, in order to safeguard the needs of whole groups with considerable inter-individual variations in their needs. Even what are called 'the minimum requirements' may still leave room for further reduction as far as some members of a group are concerned. Second, with respect to energy intake, it is possible to adapt to a low intake but only at the price of reduced physical activity, be it manual work or otherwise. There is no possibility of a similar adaptation to a lower protein intake. To quote from a recent PAG statement on the protein problem (No. 20) [12]:

'Do populations adapt to protein-calorie deficiency and thereby lower their requirements for food?'

'Not in a true sense. Adults adapt to calorie insufficiency by loss of body weight and reduction of voluntary work; children 'adapt' by retarded growth rates, as well as by decreased activity. Such 'adaptations' are unacceptable as national policy. The health and productivity of adults may be affected and for children the ultimate result may be impairment of physical and perhaps mental development.'

It should now be clear that much of what used to be called 'racial differences' in physical development is indeed caused by differences in the environment. As far as health, working

The weight of the baby: the surest measurement of health

capacity and other aspects of the 'quality of life' goals are concerned this knowledge added to what we already know about the unfavourable effect of poverty, on social, emotional and mental development, represents a mighty new challenge to work for improved conditions for the most precious possession of all nations, our children.

REFERENCES
1. Belew, M.; Jacobsson, K.; Törnell, G.; Uppsäll, L.; Zaar, B.; Vahlquist, B. Anthropometric, Clinical and Biochemical Studies in Children from Five Different Regions of Ethiopia. *J.Trop.Pediat.,* Vol.18: 246, 1972.
2. Cravioto, J; Hambraeus, L.; Vahlquist, B. (eds.). *Early Malnutrition and Mental Development.* Uppsala, Almqvist & Wiksell, 1974. (Symposia of the Swedish Nutrition Foundation XII.)
3. Dobbing, J.; Sands, J. Vulnerability of Developing Brain. IX. *Biol.Neonate,* Vol.19: 363, 1971.
4. Engsner, G. Brain Growth in Privileged and Non-Privileged Ethiopian Children. A Study Using Head Circumference Measurement, Transillumination and Ultrasonic Echo Ventriculography. *J.Trop.Pediat.,* Vol.19: 357, 1973.
5. Engsner, G.; Belete, S.; Sjögren, I.; Vahlquist, B. Brain Growth in Children with Marasmus. A Study Using Head Circumference Measurement, Transillumination and Ultrasonic Echo Ventriculography. *Upsala J.Med. Sci.,* Vol.79: 116, 1974.
6. Engsner, G.; Habte, D.; Sjögren, I.; Vahlquist, B. Brain Growth in Children with Kwashiorkor. A study Using Head Circumference Measurement, Transillumination and Ultrasonic Echo Ventriculography. *Acta Paediat. Scand.,* Vol.63: 687, 1974.
7. Engsner, G.; Woldemariam, T. Motor Nerve Conduction Velocity in Marasmus and in Kwashiorkor. *Neuropädiatrie,* Vol.5: 34, 1974.
8. Fomon, S.J. *Infant Nutrition,* 2nd ed. Philadelphia, Pa, and London, W.B. Saunders, 1974.
9. Gregg, N. McA. Congenital Cataract Following German Measles in the Mother. *Trans.Ophth.Soc.Aust.,* Vol.3: 35, 1941.
10. Greulich, W.W. Growth of Children of the Same Race Under Different Environmental Conditions. *Science,* Vol.127: 515, 1958.
11. Malnutrition and mental development. (Anonymous) *WHO Chron.,* Vol.28: 95, 1974.
12. Protein-Calorie Advisory Group of the UN System. Statement (No. 20) on the 'Protein Problem'. *PAG Bulletin,* Vol.III, No. 1: 4, 1973.
13. Stewart, R.C.; Platt, B.S. Nervous System Damage in Experimental Protein-Calorie Deficiency. In: N.S. Scrimshaw and J.S. Gordon (eds.), *Malnutrition, Learning, and Behavior,* p. 168, Cambridge, Mass., MIT Press, 1967.
14. Taylor, C.E.; DeSweemer, C. Nutrition and Infection. In: M. Rechcigl (ed.), *Food, Nutrition and Health,* p. 203. Basel, S. Karger, 1973. (Vol.16, *World Review of Nutrition and Dietetics,* ser. ed.: G.H. Bourne.)

The Cognitive Development of the African Child

E. Ayotunde Yoloye

The author considers the issues at stake in the cognitive development of the child and points out the unnatural stress that has been laid in the research field on international and interracial comparisons. More progress in the third world would be made by the study of the local setting instead, and by the supply of educative instruments, the 'implements' that have so far been lacking at a critical stage.

Introduction

The cognitive development of children has been the focus of intensive research in the past two decades. Perhaps the one person who has done most to stimulate research in this area is the Swiss psychologist Jean Piaget [16]. Piaget believes that the child's cognitive development proceeds through certain clearly defined stages from simpler to more complex levels of conceptual organization.

It is convenient to begin a discussion of the African child's cognitive development from a consideration of the stages of development proposed by Piaget for two reasons: (1) most recent research on cognitive development is based on the work of Piaget; (2) evidence is accumulating that although Piaget's studies were based mainly on Swiss children, the results are by and large valid for children in many other countries. Where there have been discrepancies, they have been mainly concerned with the age levels at which particular stages of development are attained, rather than the existence of the stages themselves.

Piaget identifies four stages of cognitive development. The first is the *sensorimotor* stage, which occupies the period from birth to 2 years. During this period, the child develops imagery, for he can at the end of this stage imitate models that are no longer present and find objects hidden in his presence. The second stage is the *preoperational* stage, which extends from 2 to about 7 years. During this period the child learns to classify things, and begins to understand causal relationships and number concepts. The third stage, *concrete operational,* extends from about 7 to about 11. During this period the child begins to use several logical operations, including: conservation; transitivity; and reversibility. The fourth stage, that of *formal operation,* is in a sense an extension of the third, but now the child is not necessarily tied down to observable events. He can operate on what is hypothetically possible. He can now operate entirely in abstract symbols.

Here we are concerned particularly with the child between birth and the age of 6. In Piaget terms, we are concerned with the child in the first two stages of cognitive development - the sensorimotor and preoperational stages. The question then is: what do we know about the African child at these two stages of development?

Research on the African child

A great deal of psychological research has been carried out in Africa, as shown by a number of bibliographies now existing on the subject [10,11,14]. However, research on the cognitive development of the African child may be regarded as still in its infancy. Many of the existing research workers have been interested in a cross-cultural comparison between African and European and North American children. With this approach and using instruments designed and standardized in western cultures, the earlier investigators came out with the rather astounding conclusion that the African is not capable of abstract thinking [3,6-8,20]. Haward & Roland indeed referred to 'The concreteness of the Nigerian's mental approach' as 'a concreteness so rigid as to produce schizophrenic signs'. These early studies tacitly suggested some genetic deficiency in the African's cognitive development.

Some subsequent studies have rightly challenged the validity of these findings as well as the assumed explanations. The first kind of challenge was directed at the instruments used in the investigations, pointing out the cultural loadings of

such instruments and the possibility of obtaining different results with instruments more relevant to the African situation. One observer [17], using animals and plants as objects for classification with Tiv children in Northern Nigeria, found evidence of ability to abstract as well as an increase in this ability with age. A second kind of challenge has been directed at the implication that deficiencies in the African cognitive development are genetic. One study [12] using the Goldstein-Scheerer cube test (which had also been used by Haward & Roland) on adolescent boys in Ghana found that boys from literate homes performed significantly better than those from illiterate homes. Further, although the children in general performed poorly on the tests by western norms, performance seemed to improve with training. Both findings point strongly to environmental factors in the African child's cognitive development. Other studies [4,5,18] introduced a new and intriguing dimension to the knowledge on the cognitive development of the African child. Geber, for example, reported on studies carried out on 308 Uganda children, 16 children in Johannesburg and 180 children in Senegal (150 tested by Falade). Using the André Thomas methods for younger children and Gesell tests for older ones, he concluded that: (1) African children showed an all-round advance of development over European standards in both motor and intellectual development; (2) the advance was greater the younger the child; (3) motor precocity is more pronounced in the first five months - adaptivity, language and personal/social relations draw level between five and seven months; (4) the level of development was that of European children two months older. Later findings indicate that the initial advance of the African child over the European child is lost in the second and third years of life.

The reports suggest that this pattern of development is related to child-rearing practices, and that the 'precocity' of the African child in the first year is largely the result of better psychological security and attention resulting from the closeness of the mother and the extended family. There is also the suggestion that after weaning the nutritional level of the child deteriorates, leading to a corresponding deterioration in motor and intellectual development. It is notable that there has been no attempt to interpret the African child's 'precocity' in genetic terms, as his deficiencies were. Abiola [1] carried these investigations a step further by comparing the intellectual development of children in illiterate traditional homes (Oje children) and those in educated westernized homes ('Elite' children), between the ages of 1 and 5. Using items from the Gesell and Merrill-Palmer scales for testing motor and perceptual development and a conceptual-verbal test of his own design, Abiola found that in general the 'Elite' children showed better performance at every age, the differences being statistically significant at 3 and 5 years for perceptual/motor development and at 2 and 5 years for conceptual-verbal development. The exception was in the first year, when the Oje children did better in the conceptual-verbal tests, although the difference was not statistically significant.

These findings lend some support to the suggestion that child-rearing practices may be responsible for the African child of Geber's studies deteriorating from precocity to deficiency compared with the European child as he grows older. The fact that the 'Elite' children in Abiola's study seem to become increasingly superior after the age of 1 suggests that a similar relationship may exist between

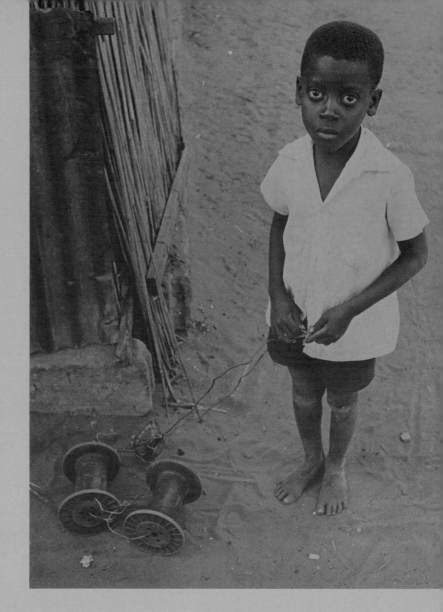

Home-made toys are better than none

children in westernized homes and those in traditional homes. The fact that children in traditional homes are not significantly superior to those in westernized homes in the first year may be an indication that the contact with loving adults and the resultant psychological security is still very strong even in westernized African homes.

The studies reported so far still leave a lot of gaps in our knowledge of the cognitive development of the African child. Some of the issues left unresolved are as follows.

Some basic issues

The first issue is one of research orientation. While international and interracial comparisons yield some useful insights, the strong emphasis that has been placed on them hitherto is questionable. Among other things it leads to such statements as that 'the African child is precocious in the first year but deficient in later years'. In either case he is portrayed as abnormal - the normal development being assumed to the European one, assessed on instruments developed in the western culture.

More progress is likely to be made if the emphasis is shifted to identifying local norms and factors that influence the level of development of individual children. Factors like age, socio-economic status, level of parents' and child's education, urban/rural environment, child-rearing practices, etc., which have been known to affect development in other cultures, should be investigated in the African setting. Too little is at present known of the ways in which these variables operate in African countries. Abiola's study is a step in the right direction. Many more along the same lines, focusing on other variables, are necessary.

A number of the studies referred to have suggested that child-rearing practices constitute an important factor in the cognitive development of the child. Already there are several comprehensive descriptions of child-rearing practices in African countries [9,13,19]. The stage is therefore sufficiently set for the next major task: investigating the effect of different aspects of these practices on cognitive development. Indications that this task may yield interesting results come from some studies going on at the Department of Social and Preventive Medicine, University of Ibadan. One study [15] has indicated that the overall development (including cognitive) of motherless babies reared in the traditional extended-family set-up is better than that of those reared in institutions like motherless babies' homes where western standards are used.

Another important factor in cognitive development identified by existing studies is education. There is no doubt, of course, that formal education fosters the cognitive development of the child. A number of issues arise therefore: (1) Is education important at an early age, e.g. pre-school? (2) If so, what kind? (3) How soon should it be embarked upon? (4) If education is deficient during this period to what extent does it affect the child's cognitive development?

In trying to answer these questions, I will discuss some theoretical considerations. One writer [2] gives an interesting angle on the role of external stimulation on cognitive development. Quoting Washburn & Howell's statement with respect to human evolution that 'The tool using, ground living, hunting way of life created the large human brain rather than a large brained man discovering certain new ways of life . . . . Size of brain, insofar as it can be measured by cranial capacity, has increased some threefold, subsequent to the use and manufacture of implements . . . ', the author postulates that 'techniques and technologies' transmitted by culture are essential ingredients in the course of cognitive growth. Human beings have three systems of processing information by which they construct models of their world, namely (a) through action (enactive representation), (b) through imagery (iconic representation), and (c) through language (symbolic representation).

The appearance of these modes of representation in the life of the child is in that order. Techniques and technologies or implement (tool) systems which promote the development of these modes of representation are respectively (a) amplifiers of human motor capacities, (b) amplifiers of sensory capacities and (c) amplifiers of human ratiocinative capacities (language systems - myth, theory and explanation).

Based on some empirical studies, the author concludes that language is the single most important factor in freeing the child from the perceptually dominant characteristics of the environment.

If these postulates are right then the course of cognitive growth is likely to be strongly affected by the nature of 'implements' existing in the culture. The improvement of these implements should lead to improvement in cognitive development. The provision of appropriate 'implements' constitutes education and, in some form, this can start from birth. The crucial question, of course, is: how adequate are the implements' existing in the traditional family set-up for development to cope with modern living? The loss of ground by the African child with respect to the European child after the first year may in fact be due to differences in the qualities of implements in the two cultures.

It is also conceivable that the critical period when these external implements become important is some time between the latter half of the first year and second year. The chances that the implements can be improved in homes in general in the near future is pretty remote. A more promising alternative is to supplement what is available in the home in formal pre-school institutions.

There is, however, a procedural problem here. The introduction of formal education in the pre-school period is relatively easy in centres of reasonable population concentration. The rural areas, however, present a special problem. It is difficult to find manpower to go into them and, in addition, it is uneconomical to send the requisite number of teachers into some of the areas having such small population concentrations.

One suggestion is that such pre-school education may be woven into mother-and-child health (MCH) centres, so that the workers, as well as being medical auxiliaries, are also people with training in the psychology of child development and pedagogy. The MCH centres will thus be miniature nursery schools: not only will they cater to the physical health of the child but they will also provide supplementary implements of all three types for promoting cognitive development.

The provision of these additional implements raises the problem of cost. If one were to think primarily of the implements of western societies, the cost would be so great as to be prohibitive. However, work done on curriculum development in Africa in recent years suggest that local, easily available materials can do as much to promote cognitive development in children as western implements can. The task is in the identification of appropriate substitutes and dissemination of information about them. One such programme - The African Primary Science Programme - is described by the present writer [21].

It is perhaps now opportune to seek a solution to the problem in the joint effort and collaboration of educational researchers, medical researchers and social workers.

REFERENCES

1. Abiola, E.T. The Nature of Intellectual Development in Nigerian Children. *Teach.Ed.*, Vol.6: 37-58, 1965.
2. Bruner, J.S. The Course of Cognitive Growth. In: N.S. Endler, L.R. Boulter and H. Osser (eds.), *Contemporary Issues in Developmental Psychology.* London, Holt, Rinehart & Winston, 1970.
3. Carothers, J.C. *The African Mind in Health and Disease.* Geneva, World Health Organization, 1953.
4. Geber, M. The Psycho-Motor Development of African Children in the First Year and the Influence of Maternal Behaviour. *J.Soc.Psychol.*, Vol.47: 185-95, 1958.
5. Geber, M.; Dean, R.F.A. Le Développement Psychomoteur et Somatique des Jeunes Enfants Africains en Ouganda. *Courrier,* Vol.14: 425,437, 1964.
6. Haward, L.C.R.; Roland, W.A. Some Intercultural Differences on the Draw-a-Man Test. Good Enough Scores. *Man,* Vol.54: 86-8, 1944.
7. ——; ——. Some Inter-cultural Differences on the Draw-a-Man Test. Pt II: Matchover Scores. *Man,* Vol.55: 27-9, 1955.
8. ——; ——. Some Inter-cultural Differences on the Draw-a-Man Test. Pt III: Conclusion. *Man,* Vol.55: 40-2, 1955.
9. Henderson, R.N.; Henderson, H. *An Outline of Traditional Onitsha Ibo Socialization.* Ibadan, University of Ibadan, 1966. (Institute of Education, Occasional publ. No.5.)
10. Hoorweg, J.C.; Marais, H.C. *Psychology in Africa. A Bibliography.* Leyden, Afrika Studien Centrum, 1969.
11. Irvine, S.H.; Sanders, J.T.; Klingelhofer, E.L. *Human Behaviour in Africa: A Bibliography of Psychological and Related Writings.* London, 1970. (Mimeo.)
12. Jahoda, G. Assessment of Abstract Behaviour in a Non-Western Culture. *J.Abnorm. & Soc.Psychol.*, Vol.53: 237-43, 1956.
13. Kaye, B. *Bringing Up Children in Ghana.* London, Allen & Unwin, 1962.
14. Klingelhofer, E.L. *A Bibliography of Psychological Research and Writings on Africa.* Uppsala, Scandinavian Institute of African Studies, 1967.
15. Oyemade, A. The Care of Motherless Babies in Nigeria. Glasgow, 1973. (MD thesis.)
16. Piaget, J. *The Psychology of Intelligence.* New York, NY, Harcourt, 1950.
17. Price-Williams, D.R. Abstract and Concrete Modes of Classification in a Primitive Soceity. *Br.J.Ed.Psychol.*, Vol.32: 50-61, 1962.
18. Senecal, J.; Falade, S.A. Développement Psychomoteur de l'Enfant Africain au Cours de la Première Année. *Bull.Med. de l'AOF,* Vol.1: 300-9, 1956.
19. Uka, N. *Growing Up in Nigerian Culture.* Ibadan, University of Ibadan, 1966. (Institute of Education Occasional publ. No.6.)
20. Wintringer, G. Considérations sur l'Intelligence du Noir Africain. *Revue Psychol. des Peuples,* Vol.10: 37-55, 1955.
21. Yoloye, E.A. The African Primary Science Programme. *J.Sci.Teach.Ass. Nigeria,* Vol.9, No.1, 1970.

The Myth of Precocity

Western researchers have sought to establish some inherent differences between Africans and Europeans or North Americans. The earliest investigators were frequently content to fall back on overtly racialist assertions, without seeking to justify their attitudes by scientific method. More recently, refinements of approach have led to the hypothesis of precocity, in brief, to the idea that African children are more advanced in development at birth than European children and that this advance endures until the age of 1 1/2 to 3 years, after which the relative positions are reversed. Considerable weight has been attached to this theory, which emerged mainly from work in Uganda in the 1950s by Geber [2, 4], preceded by Theunissen [5] and Falade [1].

Through an exhaustive review of the material available, Warren [6] has made it clear that, because of the unsatisfactory nature of the majority of studies carried out:

1. African infant precocity has not been satisfactorily demonstrated. Only four studies have been carried out in a satisfactory manner. Of these four, two studies do not support the theory of precocity; the two that do support the theory carry the defect of making comparisons with available western norms and not with samples of European babies taken by the same investigator.
2. Africans have not been shown conclusively to fall systematically below western levels in late infancy and early childhood.

The main source of generalizations about African infant development, the work of Geber, compares most unfavourably with at least half the other reports reviewed. 'Citations (often erroneous) from a single brief and inadequate paper [3] have usually been the basis for generalizations on African infant development.' Warren's conclusion was that, if anything, differences of social milieu provided a more sensible basis for research, inasmuch as results related to social level did show consistency whereas there could be no clear conclusion about results of research into African precocity.

Writers like Jensen and Eysenck, having accepted uncritically the findings of Geber & Dean, went on to infer from the supposed hereditary early precocity the likelihood of genetically determined African intellectual inferiority at full maturity. Practically speaking, the possibility of valid and definitive cross-cultural conclusions is still remote and the pursuit of the study of precocity intraculturally would appear to be an irrelevance when compared with the scope for research based on the analysis of specific aspects of care, rearing and experience in any milieu.

REFERENCES

1. Faladé, S. *Contribution à une Etude sur le Développement de l'Enfant d'Afrique Noire.* Paris, Foulon, 1955.
2. Geber, M. Développement Psycho-moteur de l'Enfant Africain. *Courrier,* Vol.6:17-29, 1956.
3. - - - - -. The Psychomotor Development of African Children in the First Year, and the Influence of Maternal Behaviour. *J.Soc.Psychol.,* Vol.47: 185-95, 1958.
4. Geber, M.; Dean, R.F.A. Psychomotor Development in African Children: The Effects of Social Class and the Need for Improved Tests. *Bull. WHO,* Vol.18: 471-6, 1958.
5. Theunissen, K.B. A Preliminary Comparative Study of the Development of Motor Behavior in European and Bantu Children up to the Age of One Year. Durban, Natal University College, 1948. (Unpubl. Master's thesis.)
6. Warren, Neil. African Infant Precocity. *Psychol.Bull.,* Vol. 78, No.5: 353-67, 1972.

The Problem of Socialization in Africa

T. Peter Omari

Children are much desired in the traditional African family. This may be, as Peter Omari points out, partly because large families are the best defence where infant mortality is high and where so much work is still done by children. Governments still accept that the welfare of the child should remain primarily the responsibility of parents and families and this attitude will need to change if greater progress is to be made in child care.

Compared with other living creatures, man in infancy is the most helpless creature and takes the longest time to mature. While most other animals are animated into action on their own or with very little help from their mothers soon after birth, human babies need intensive care and protection and gradual tutoring in order that they can be assimilated into their environment.

We are all agreed - mothers, fathers, doctors, welfare workers, judicial persons and politicians, etc. - that babies and children need special care and protection. How this is to be done - and how to respond to the health and social needs of the child - are difficult questions.

We are concerned here with the manner and the process by which the child, which at birth can only be considered as a 'bundle of tendencies', acquires a social self as it develops physically and mentally, comes to perceive role requirements, and adopts attitudes concerning its own roles and the roles of other persons. This process of socialization is also concerned with the norms and the culture of the society into which the child has been born. These norms and culture patterns shape its upbringing and determine, very often, how well the child will grow up physically and mentally. The social and cultural milieu is also important in any programme of child care and child health - especially in rural communities.

The process of socialization

The child begins to react to its environment even before it is born. At birth, the way in which a child is manipulated and fondled by its mother or its nurse, including the enormously important social and physical contacts involved in feeding and other physical ministrations, constitutes the child's first experience with social influences. The social behaviour which we call love and affection may be quite essential to the survival and well-being of babies in one culture but it may play a different role in another and be expressed in different forms.

The child acquires the habits, attitudes and beliefs of the group to which it belongs chiefly through contacts with other persons. The development of self comes when a child acquires language. Until then its social development is similar to that of all social animals. With the development of language and the self-consciousness and social consciousness which it makes possible, together with that wide range of phenomena that is designated by the word 'mind', the distinctively social characteristics of an individual are born. In this connexion the primary group to which the child belongs is crucial.

Socialization is a continuing process by which the group develops self-restraints. Where socialization fails, the demands upon the group's sanction system may be severe. Fragmentation, conflict and the development of subgroup social structures (or subcultures) are likely to result. The process of socialization is therefore essential if society is to function cohesively and if the individual is to develop into a whole person and make a positive contribution to the social and economic development of the country.

The cultural basis for socialization
The culture of the society, being the soil in which a child grows, needs to be studied carefully for traits, patterns of thought and behaviour which will promote growth and the proper development of the child. It has been pointed out that doctors and hospitals have tended largely to cure disease and not to promote health. Good health is everybody's need and activity to promote it should be rooted in the everyday life of the people. We therefore need to analyse aspects of African culture that bear upon child development, and subsequently, to discuss how these attitudes and behaviour patterns may be marshalled in support of programmes for child health and child care. In doing so it must be pointed out that African society is both dualistic and complex. It is more appropriate to speak of the modern and traditional sectors of society, and of 'societies' rather than 'society', for within a given society may be found, vertically, groups that are to a greater or lesser degree quite westernized or 'emancipated' [1] as well as illiterate peasants and tradition-bound groups and, on the horizontal plane, diversified groups and cultures. Generalizations are dangerous and I have therefore restricted my comments to the background of Ghana, drawing on, in particular, Barrington Kaye [2].

Attitudes to children, pregnancy and childbirth. Africans generally have a positive attitude towards having children. Barrington Kaye reported that married couples in Ghana commonly wanted children and valued them more highly than wealth. They did so because children were greatly valued for help in the house and on the farm, to serve visitors, to support their parents and be their heirs. Girls as well as boys were of economic value since they were a means for the parents of obtaining money and cattle through the bride-price. Children in Ghana were thus a source of social prestige and parents of ten children or twins were greatly respected, and sometimes believed to be holy.

Thus children add to social prestige, remove the stigma of barrenness and mean more hands on the farm, in some way contributing to the happiness of parents, especially if they are boys. Sterility and barrenness are consequently decried and abhorred for various reasons. Although pregnancy is looked forward to, it is often dreaded for the many cases of death in childbirth, especially in the case of first babies. There are many taboos associated with pregnancy, some of which concern sexual intercourse during the period and types of foods to be eaten or avoided.

Women in Africa are expected to carry out their normal duties from the onset of pregnancy to mere days before delivery. These include farming, food-gathering, housekeeping, preparation of food, especially for the husband, and fetching water. Women have been known to deliver while chopping firewood on farms and while returning home from farms with large loads on their heads or backs.

'Morning sickness' is a Victorian luxury from which an African woman seldom has the privilege to suffer. But a pregnant woman is respected and protected from encounters with unpleasant experiences. In most African societies it is thought that she should not look at ugly animals or persons, or be scared by any, for fear that the baby will be born with such an appearance.

Childbirth is a critical period for most pregnant women and a woman in labour is said to lie 'between life and death'. Women are generally expected to bear the pains of childbirth courageously and shouts of pain are generally considered signs of weakness. Since there is hardly any medical assistance, traditional midwives - usually a grandmother - assist with births. When no complications arise, births proceed safely; otherwise dire consequences follow for both mother and child.

A husband is not generally allowed to attend the birth of his child. But in Teshie (Ga) in Ghana a woman who begins to have difficulty with delivery is often urged to shout the name of the father - the real father - and this is often thought to cause the child to be delivered with greater ease. Women who have never given birth are also not allowed to witness the delivery for fear of being scared into not having babies when they marry. Various rites attend to babies after delivery.

Age and sex. Age and sex are two of the most significant variables in African culture. Sibling age is important. The elders are revered and what they say both in the home and in the community is taken as literal truth. Because of this emphasis on the elders, it has not been possible in the traditional African context to make the child the vehicle of an innovative process. This has long been a dilemma for educationists and health workers: a young student of a modern educational system may have learned what there is to know about health and agricultural practices, but if these go against the seasoned beliefs of the elders he stands in danger of being ostracized for practising them himself in their midst, or he faces grave difficulties in attempting to persuade them to the new view. The approach can become more easy with equals in age and in sex.

African politics are generally male-dominated even when the society is matrilineal. As a result, greater value is attached to having, raising, educating and promoting males and activities for males, than for females. While a female head of household in a matrilineal society may order men about in domestic matters, it is generally not accepted that women should advise on important questions. As a result of this, and in modernizing societies, boys receive more education than girls; boys will be accorded more privileges than girls, while parental love and affection may be displayed more openly to girls than to boys for fear of 'spoiling' the boy, who is expected to grow into manhood as a 'tough', unemotional and brave person.

Girls are expected to please and serve men and are therefore brought up with greater 'love' and 'affection' than boys. Girls are also trained to work hard, for in African societies the women do most of the work both at home and on the farm. On the whole, parents tend to favour the baby among the children more than the older ones; the first-born and the last-born; those who are named after well-loved relatives; and those whose delivery was attended with excessive pains. But older children are entitled to the respect and obedience of their juniors, and have the right to the first helping of meat or fish, especially when these are small.

From childhood into adulthood. An African child does not normally acquire identity by the mere accident of birth. Although African parents are child-conscious, bitter experience with the vagaries of life that often deprive them of the joy of childbirth also teach them to be fatalistic and to hold up demonstrations of affection until there is some degree of certainty that a child will live. Parents who have lost successive children might even be forced to deform or deface a newborn baby in the hope of saving it from the 'forces of evil'. A baby enters upon adulthood with the performance of puberty or similar rites or upon attaining a prescribed age, generally 16-18. Not much has been made of the various age groups or stages in life and this is largely because they have not served any particular functions. Like all technologically undeveloped societies, traditional African culture has developed on such lines as to reduce the exigencies of living to a minimum. It has thus sufficed mainly to designate periods of childhood, youth (coming of age) and old age. But these broad classifications or designations should present no barrier to programmes calling for more detailed activities on behalf of young people. Precise ages may not be known but

subdivisions in these categories are possible. An infant may be said to have become a family member as such when it has come of age and can assume independent responsibilities, in spite of the fact that it is expected long before then to have been making a contribution to the economic life of the family.

Cognition and learning in the African child. A child becomes a person when it acquires the power of language. But long before that it perceives, feels, understands and can communicate feelings and desires. Since there have been no schools, tutoring and learning through observation and experience play a large role in the socialization of the African child. In matrilineal, largely matrilocal, societies, all children live with their mothers until about the age of 6 or 7, when the boys transfer to the men's places of residence. This is so even in many patrilineal societies. Within the more modern sectors of society, where families are more nuclear than extended, a child has an opportunity to grow up in a mixed setting in which he or she can observe relationships between a father and mother on a continuous basis. This, of course, influences the position that a child holds in the love and affection of parents and vice versa.

Rights, love and affection of children. As we have learned, children have no rights until they reach adulthood. They are, in a sense, 'non-persons'. But the Ghanaian proverb that 'every one is royalty in his family' is also an indication of the sense of security that a family - the extended family and the clan - confers on a child. Rights he may not have. But parental position is of utmost importance to a growing child. In the past, children of royalties, for example, have held royal positions both at court and in society. Similarly those of low birth must later show some prowess which is the only means of mitigating their low social position acquired at birth. So,

a child grows up in the aura of his or her parental position until it is old enough to acquire an individual personality of its own or to diminish its inherited position. Inheritance is, of course, a natural aspect of African social structure.

Love and affection are, however, more personal. Africans are not generally known to demonstrate love, especially in public. Such would be equated with familiarity, which in Africa more than elsewhere is thought to breed contempt. Love can also be severe - especially in the case of children. Because parents want their children to grow up into responsible citizens, to show love and affection to a child is disapproved and it is often considered that to spare the rod is to spoil the child. It is therefore very difficult to determine from mere observation how an African parent loves his child. Often, however, children understand and behave as they are expected to, knowing that they owe to their parents responsible behaviour.

Being older also confers special honour on parents, which the culture enjoins children to recognize and respect. As one aspect of their socialization, boys grow up into adulthood demonstrating affection to neither wife nor children in the sense that it is understood in Western societies; but through deeds and other performances they manage to communicate the same.

On life and death. The hazards of life have taught the African to be fatalistic in his attitude to it. Death of children - at least up to the age of 1 - is seldom mourned. Traditional African society is seldom faced with the dilemma of saving the mother or the baby in childbirth for example. It would always be life for the mother. A Ghanaian proverb has it that 'it is better to save the pot than break the pot attempting to save the water it contains'. One can always go for another pot of water, it is thought. In many African societies it was the traditional practice to examine all newly born babies for any deformations so that a judgement could be made as to whether or not they should be allowed to live. It was generally considered that the fittest should survive, so that they could cope with the rigours of life. It has been observed, in fact, that in many clinics and hospitals babies are seldom brought for care when sick, only when they are dying or after traditional efforts at cure have failed.

From the age of 1 to 2 years, after most of the 'unfit' had died off, life for the baby was somewhat stable until after the weaning period, when malnutrition and infectious diseases combined to take a toll. At this age, of course, death becomes an agony either because of the attachment formed for the baby, because of the cost of having brought it up so far or because of loss of potential economic benefit. Also, from this age onwards a child begins to assume a personality and its loss is much felt.

Child care: focus for planning

We may now consider some of the factors already mentioned, in order to see how they promote or impede better child health and child care.

Attitudes to children, pregnancy and childbirth. Because children are desired in themselves, family planning has not acquired the significance it should have in many African countries and has, unfortunately, come to be associated almost exclusively with birth control. But the wider aspect of family welfare and development is now gaining ground. The Economic Commission for Africa is now explaining the welfare basis for family planning and is beginning to achieve some recognition for this point of view. Birth control itself should not be difficult for Africans to accept if the basic cultural factor is explained, for many of the cultural practices

inherent in the marriage custom and the practice of breast-feeding included built-in birth-control aspects.

Departments of social welfare and rural development, far from being only remotely concerned with health and educational child-care programmes, must closely integrate these into any plans for rural communities. For example, one of the most difficult periods in the life of many rural women is the period of childbirth. Since many governmental facilities do not reach into rural communities and since, as we have learned, many grandmothers are traditional midwives, any programme that raises the level of knowledge of hygiene and delivery for village grandmothers will go a long way to reduce perinatal wastage. The rudimentary knowledge required can well be imparted by social-welfare and rural-development workers in women's and/or adult education or adult-literacy programmes as much as in health-education programmes under the auspices of the ministry of health.

It is also common knowledge that herbalists treat mothers and children at delivery as well as thereafter. If herbalists and practitioners of native medicine can be taught to undertake vaccinations or organized (as in the case of Ghana, for example) and given adult education and other courses that will raise their art a little higher than already obtains, some progress would have been made towards improved rural health care, at least for the perinatal period.

Age and sex. In any health-education programme, the age factor has to be recognized and an effort made not to take it lightly. The reason many educational programmes fail in the rural areas is because the innovators are not old enough to counsel mothers and fathers. To get around this age barrier, elders in the communities are often given in-service training courses and sent out to accompany innovators who might be young. The introduction is made by the older 'assistant' before the young innovator takes over. A similar barrier operates in sex: to send someone of the opposite sex to discuss the subject, when this is forbidden by tradition, is to court disaster.

From childhood into adulthood. The (traditional) eating habits of a community must be observed with great insight before nutrition education is embarked upon. For example, in some communities children must not eat eggs and certain portions of meat or fowl, usually the most nutritious. Certain of these taboos extend even to the women. Generally, adults eat before children can eat. The sum of all this is that adults eat the most nutritious portions of the food at hours usually late for children and for good digestion before sleep. Seldom do parents and children sit down at table together and share the available meal and when the children sit down to their own meal, the youngest is always at a disadvantage because he must compete with the older ones.

Nothing short of revolutionary teaching will change this eating habit. One of the sources of the tradition of not eating with anyone but an equal is in the widespread proverb that 'if you eat with a dog, you must expect to be licked at the mouth by one'. It is time for parents - especially husbands and fathers - to be taught to accept the difference between their dogs and their children and to control their fears of rudeness from their children if the practice of not eating with their children is to be abandoned.

On the burden of womanhood. Women in Africa carry the greatest burden of society, and in the socialization of the African child, they exercise the greatest influence. Nevertheless, they receive less attention in the development effort than men. They must therefore be given the greatest opportunity to raise their standard of living as well as to play an active role in the social and economic programmes of their countries. From infancy to his or her maturation, it is the woman who teaches the child to live, to love, to learn, to grow in good health and to assume responsibilities - well before her husband or the child's father takes over any responsibility for these. Dr Kwegyr Aggrey long ago summed up the weight of this responsibility when he said: 'You educate a man, you educate an individual; you educate a woman, you educate a nation.' Although husbands should be integrated into any educational programmes for the health and welfare of the child, it is obvious that any programme that does not recognize the position of the woman in the African society is doomed to rapid failure.

Planning for socialization
The family and the community - the primary groups - are not the only institutions with responsibility to ensure or promote socialization or child development. Society has the greater responsibility to ensure the adequacy and continued success of facilities for socialization. Governments are increasingly participating in the process. Socialization, although not synonymous with child development, is conterminous with it. Both must proceed hand in hand in order to ensure the child's all-round development. In planning for the socialization and development of the child - a comparatively recent concept - it is best to think of the whole child in relation to his family and to society, as well as to conceive the process as an integrated effort. Upon this child (person) must be concentrated the concerted effort of various disciplines or functional programmes. Additionally, attention must be given to other related areas which although not directly concerned with the child nevertheless are crucial to its successful upbringing: services for the betterment of the child's primary and secondary environment; services that will equip parents

and family to discharge their tasks competently (employment opportunities, adult literacy and community development services, education, women's programmes, health and sanitation facilities); and a wholesome social environment. The plan itself must have an objective and this objective must derive from defined or perceived needs. The requirements of African rural or traditional society do not always fully correspond to these needs, which have been better defined by the paediatricians, public-health officers, nutritionists, urban and rural health planners, educationists, social workers and others who attended the Addis Ababa seminar. These have been grouped into a five-point child-care package that now requires official endorsement and implementation. Unfortunately, African governments seem to take the view that the greater responsibility for the welfare of the child rests on parents and families and that their own responsibility lies mainly in supplementing this effort. None the less, even if the child is not seen as a productive or political force, and if the value of a large-scale effort is ill understood, governments will have to change their attitudes if a greater result is to be achieved in the region.

REFERENCES
1. Omari, T.P. *Marriage Guidance for Young Ghanaians.* Edinburgh, Nelson, 1962.
2. Kaye, Barrington. *Bringing Up Children in Ghana.* London, Allen & Unwin, 1962.

The school garden: education for living

The Dilemmas

Dilemma   (dile·ma, dəi-), sb. A choice between two (or several) alternatives, which are equally unfavourable
Oxford English Dictionary

Dilemma   (*di* twice plus *lemma* assumption). A situation involving choice between equally unsatisfactory alternatives
Webster's Dictionary

Beginning at the Beginning

Adam's was the first recorded dilemma, but these familiar, usually unwelcome and complex situations have continued to hinder and confuse decision-making. Men and women do manage, however, to surmount these complexities: they make decisions, follow them through and find ways out of what seem to be overwhelming positions. Such conflicting situations constantly confront health workers everywhere, and much more acutely in developing countries with their limited resources, where the problem is often compounded by a bewildering variety of possible solutions, such that choosing between alternatives may be as confusing as the problem itself. We need to know what precepts will help them to make decisions and to make the best or most effective use of resources at hand.

Paediatricians who are fortunate enough to work in departments like the Ethio-Swedish Paediatric Clinic, that function well and follow progressive ideals and policies, are encouraged to expand their outlook and turn attention to·the issues and problems involved in child care in its broadest sense. Thus, common questions raised and debated in open discussions range from those pertaining to the hospital situation itself -

*Why did we admit that child, when to treat so severe a case of protein-energy
malnutrition at that stage was useless?*
Aren't we overemphasizing treatment for newborns?
*Wouldn't that infant have survived if the mother had only been admitted before the
onset of labour?*
If only that midwife had told us in time, could we not have saved the child?

to matters of economy -

If we admit this child for surgery, will we then have money left for vaccine?
What is the cost of maintaining a bed at our hospital?
What does it cost to treat meningitis?

to social and environmental implications -

*Why should we support this WHO immunization schedule when those preventable
diseases are not at the root of our high infant mortality rate?*
*Why are the aid organizations so concerned about smallpox eradication, when the
death rate in malnutrition is one hundredfold greater?*
*Isn't it nonsensical to teach this mother the benefits of eggs and milk, when she
cannot even afford water?*
*Why does that father refuse family guidance, when anyone can see that one more
child will almost destroy the mother, not to mention the family economy?*
Does no one in the family realize that this child needs love and attention?
Should we advise this mother to buy cow's milk or to dig a latrine?
Shouldn't we approach the father instead? After all, he is the breadwinner.
*How has this poor and illiterate mother been able to bring up such a well-nourished
child?*

In addition there are questions that are just as realistic:

Is it right to keep the majority of the country's paediatric experts in the capital?

Why has this child with such a harmless sickness been referred to this specialist centre?
Why are we so uninterested in teaching when it is the best means of spreading our knowledge?
Why do we find it so meaningless and unrewarding to sit on an MCH committee?
Can't more realistic nutrition education be given in schools?
Why is the government investing so much in agriculture when, after all, you cannot farm unless you are healthy?

In all cases decisions must be made.

We must make up our minds. We have to choose.
We must find the criteria and only then shall we be on the way to solving our dilemma.

There are, of course, no perfect answers to our questions. Health workers, social workers, educationists and planners throughout Africa are familiar with them, and they are struggling to find workable ways of solving them. For solutions have to be found if there is to be a reasonable chance of development within the foreseeable future.

Bryant (1969) has opened up the question:

The moral issues involved in curing individual patients are well known and often discussed. But the moral issues associated with providing health care for large numbers of people, particularly when resources are severely limited, are less well appreciated. The lack of understanding of these issues - indeed, the failure to recognize that they exist - is a serious obstacle to improving health care, whether it is being provided by a government, health service, university or church.

Most health workers in subSaharan Africa have been trained to practise medicine according to a conscious or unconscious cognizance of the Hippocratic oath.

Those who make
policy decisions

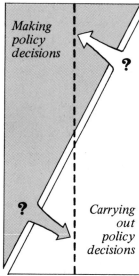

Those who carry out
policy decisions

**Policy-makers and
practitioners:
the dilemma of
value judgements
and action (after
Grundy and Reinke,1973)**

However, assuming responsibility for giving optimum health care to all the people in one's area is also a basic obligation. A dilemma can arise when a health worker has to choose between two or more ways of acting in a health-care situation, when the optimum alternative is not always obvious. Similarly, a more implicit dilemma may present itself when the principle of doing one's utmost to save the individual patient's life conflicts with the wider issue of serving all the people.

Such dilemmas may seem quite different to the health worker face to face with real people and to the planner who deals with them as statistical abstractions, to be catered for from his desk. If we accept the central question - whom to serve when all cannot be served - we cannot avoid taking into consideration the intrinsic values of human life. We must assume that everyone has the right to life. We cannot build on any other assumption. This imperative has been recognized by the United Nations, which adopted in 1948 through its General Assembly the Universal Declaration of Human Rights, containing the following key affirmation: 'Everyone has the right to life . . .'

The meaning of life presents problems of semantics that can only be confronted by the philosopher but the value of life in terms of quality is more amenable to immediate discussion by negative definition. Thus it is reasonable to assume that no one living would prefer to remain undernourished, crippled or deprived of the possibility of maximizing their life potential. The Universal Declaration also clarified the value of life to which man has a right in this sense by affirming positively that everyone has the right to a standard of living adequate for the health and well-being of himself and of his family, including food, clothing, housing and medical care and necessary social services and that motherhood and childhood are entitled to special care and assistance. Health itself is defined in the Constitution of the World Health Organization as a 'state of complete physical, mental and social well-being and not merely the absence of disease or infirmity'.

The chief implication of such definitions is their universality - that all people should enjoy the benefits of life and health. The corollary is that enjoyment of good health and the other social desiderata by a minority cannot be considered an adequate achievement by the community even of minimal goals well below the target defined for health by the World Health Organization.

The distance that separates the achievement of universal good health and the present state of imperfection is the area of dilemma and we have already seen some of the unavoidable questions that arise. The four examples that follow, that are inspired by an earlier presentation by Bryant (1969), present some of the dilemmas in a more concrete context. The background to these examples is the Ethiopian health-care system and each is described from the standpoint of a staff member of the Ethio-Swedish Paediatric Clinic, illustrating a problem at a different level of the system and seeking guidance at that level. (The Ethiopian term, 'health officer', is equivalent to the perhaps more widely used medical assistant'; 'dresser' to 'health assistant'; and 'community nurse' to 'public-health nurse'.)

What the Dilemmas Are: Four Examples by Level

1 The Rural Health Centre

Background The health centre is comparatively isolated, 200 kilometres from the nearest provincial hospital and accessible only to four-wheel-drive vehicles. It has a few beds for in-patients, but no surgical facilities and no telephone. It is served by a health officer, a community nurse, a sanitarian and two auxiliaries, whose salaries consume most of the limited budget. Drug supply is irregular; penicillin and sulphonamides are the only available antibiotics, although stocks of vaccines for smallpox and other diseases are adequate. There is a land-rover, though it is forbidden to transport patients in it. Only seventy-five litres of petrol remain at the time in question.

Situation Reports of a smallpox outbreak with already two deaths are brought eighty kilometres from a village of 1,000 inhabitants, none of whom has been vaccinated. Of the fifty patients seeking treatment at the health centre, four children with diarrhoea are in urgent need of intravenous infusion to replace lost body fluids. A week's course of penicillin has failed to cure pneumonia in the son of the village chief. A woman has been in obstructed labour for twenty-four hours; regular foetal heartbeats can still be heard.

Dilemma *At least two lines of action present themselves:*
A The health officer has instructions that preventive activities take priority over curative ones. However, if the sanitarian takes the land-rover and deals with the smallpox epidemic, the only means of communication with the provincial hospital will be lost. There is intravenous fluid enough to treat only two children, and the other two in need may die. Which ones? The woman in labour will probably lose her baby if she cannot receive surgical attention soon. The village chief commands authority and respect in the village. If his son dies, the withdrawal of his father's support could jeopardize the future activities of the centre.

B Although it would be against instructions, the land-rover could take the more needy patients to the provincial hospital. But there is room for only three. Who should be left behind? The health officer must decide - himself. He cannot ask his superiors. A return trip to the hospital will take two days, and attempts to control the smallpox epidemic will be seriously delayed. It may spread and more may die.

2 | The Provincial Hospital

Background A doctor with limited surgical experience, two nurses and three dressers are the only medically trained staff at this hospital in a provincial town of 50,000 inhabitants, eighty kilometres from the capital. The limited drug stocks include only the more simple antibiotics such as penicillin and some intravenous fluids, although none suitable for treating dehydration due to diarrhoea.

Situation On this particular morning the provincial medical officer is attending a conference in the capital. One nurse and a dresser are attending about one hundred mothers and children in the recently introduced MCH clinic. Attendance rates have been increasing and the mothers are showing more interest in the vaccination and nutrition education programmes included. Their continued confidence is essential to its ultimate success.

The other nurse has singled out as the most urgent among seventy patients awaiting treatment two children with diarrhoea in need of fluid replacement intravenously and a semi-conscious man whose condition indicates meningitis. His relatives report that several neighbours have similar symptoms. A 12-year-old motor-accident victim shows signs of severe intra-abdominal bleeding, necessitating immediate surgery.

A land-rover arrives, bringing a boy with pneumonia, a child seriously dehydrated with diarrhoea and a woman in obstructed labour, all referred from an outlying health centre. The foetal heartbeats are irregular, and only an urgent caesarian section might save the baby.

Dilemma *Are the critical surgical cases to be treated before the equally urgent medical ones? And, if so, does the unborn child take precedence over the accident victim? The delay of an hour and a half before the second operation could be commenced would almost certainly cause the death of either. To operate would withdraw the services of the doctor, a nurse and a dresser from any other duties for many hours. How should the remaining nurse divide her attention between the MCH clinic, important for its long-term benefits, the serious medical cases and the multitude of 'not-so-ill' patients who must nevertheless be attended? Should a nurse or dresser be removed from the hospital to investigate the possible neighbourhood meningitis outbreak? Would the doctor be justified in refraining from operating so that a greater number of lives might possibly be saved if he were to treat the medical cases, investigate the meningitis and treat it in its early stages, and carry on the vaccination and education activities of the MCH clinic?*

Because there is no fluid to treat the severely dehydrated patients or modern, broad-spectrum antibiotics to treat pneumonia, how can these patients reach the central hospital in the capital were he to refer them there?

3 | The Central Hospital

Background This hospital - the only children's hospital in the city - has ninety beds and a large out-patient department handling 300 visits daily. In this dry season diarrhoea is extremely common, and the patient-load is maximal. Because of the limited number of beds, it has been the practice to administer replacement fluids to dehydrated children in the out-patient department. The majority of patients are unable to pay for treatment, and at the present time the budgetary allocation for drugs is almost consumed.

Situation The physician in charge has admitted several emergency patients and only one unoccupied bed remains in the wards. The out-patient department staff are administering intravenous fluid to dehydrated children who take up all available couch and bench space. The rate of flow of the fluid must be constantly checked and takes the full time of the staff.

Now some additional emergency cases arrive:

1. Four small children with diarrhoea need urgent intravenous infusion.
2. A girl with meningitis requires treatment with intravenous antibiotics.
3. An 18-month-old boy, severely undernourished, presents with pneumonia and diarrhoea after measles. His mother has no family in the city and no means of income.
4. A boy with pneumonia has been referred from a provincial hospital. His parents have no relatives in the city and have spent their last money on bus fares. The physician realizes that, if the boy is to survive, costly antibiotics are needed.

Dilemma *It seems impossible to accommodate four more children in the out-patient department where it is already proving beyond the capabilities of the staff to manage the number of infusions already in progress. Can these children be refused treatment? Only one of the other three children can be admitted. Is it ethically justified to admit the boy with pneumonia and treat him with expensive drugs, when the same amount of money could save the lives of fifteen other children? It will probably cost one-tenth of that amount to cure the girl with meningitis, and her parents can even pay the admission fee! But, can the boy be refused treatment? Where should the parents turn? The undernourished child with post-measles infection will require a long hospital stay - perhaps eight weeks. Does it make sense to let this child occupy a bed for this period, depriving six other children of hospital treatment, and knowing that, after discharge, his mother will be unable to provide adequate nutritional care?*

The University Hospital

Background The hospital's neonatal unit can accommodate ten sick newborns or low-birth-weight infants, and has an adjacent room for the care of the mothers. The staff is fairly experienced, and there are two good incubators. But emergency laboratory services are very limited. The unit is heavily criticized as it is the most expensive service run by the hospital, both as regards staff time and budget.

Situation A 35-year-old woman with leprosy is delivered by caesarian section of a boy, her sixth child and first son. The baby, weighing only three kilos, does not breathe at birth, and a paediatrician is called to assist. After prolonged artificial respiration, spontaneous breathing commences; but, as the infant's general condition is unsatis – factory, he is admitted to the neonatal unit for observation. The baby is in a critical condition, inactive, unresponsive to any stimulus, and breathing irregularly. There is a large swelling on the head due to bleeding caused by birth trauma. The severe general weakness indicates a degree of brain damage, but at 12 hours of age he looks slightly better. A chest X-ray later in the day shows extensive pneumonia, and so treatment with the appropriate antibiotics is commenced. Some improvement is observed, but he remains in an incubator and intravenous infusion is continued.

At 48 hours, breathing stops, necessitating artificial respiration with continuous oxygen administration. This is followed the same day by convulsions, so appropriate sedation is given. On the third day he looks much better, but cannot suck when feeding is attempted. Nourishment is given through a tube and is tolerated well. The convulsions are less frequent and breathing is satisfactory. However, the child's muscular tone is poor, and his mother is notified of his doubtful prognosis. On the sixth day he appears yellow; the bilirubin in his blood is at a critical level, and an exchange blood transfusion is carried out. This is repeated next day when his condition again deteriorates.

All goes reasonably well until the 15th day when he develops watery diarrhoea. Stool culture reveals infection by an organism sensitive only to one of the most modern antibiotics. His condition rapidly worsens and the treatment, though expensive, is initiated. The diarrhoea is controlled, but the baby still has to be tube-fed. He has occasional convulsions, but his limbs are now firm. The mother is transferred from the obstetrical ward to the 'mother's room'. She shows no interest in her infant, and leaves next day. The baby at 6 weeks of age remains inactive unless stimulated, is underweight and does not suck properly. It is now obvious that the chances of a full recovery are almost non-existent.

Dilemma *When should one stop treatment? Should it have stopped a few minutes after birth when the baby failed to respond immediately to resuscitation, or when convulsions started, or when the jaundice was noticed, or when the diarrhoea developed? Or now? Until when should this supportive care continue at the expense of other sick babies and their chances for treatment?*

The Participants Speak

The discussion contributions that follow are a selection of those made at the Addis Ababa seminar. No summary of the discussion as a whole is included here but an effort has been made to include contributions from as many speakers as possible. The comments have not been revised by the contributors and the ultimate responsibility for their presentation therefore rests with the editors.

Adetokunbo O. Lucas
(Professor of Preventive and Social Medicine, University of Ibadan, Nigeria)

For me the last case has been one of the easiest, because, not being a paediatrician, I don't think I would have got that far with it. The other situations are, I think, quite familiar to many doctors and ones which none of us has been able to solve. It is, perhaps, very similar to the situation of the man who went to a toy-shop to buy a modern educational toy for his child, and he saw many different ones. But the man said, 'Come and buy this very latest one; it is the very best thing we have got. It is a three-dimensional jigsaw puzzle and the thing about it is this - that, no matter which way the child puts it together, it is wrong'. And this, itself, trains him for dealing with this kind of situation!

It is quite clear that, no matter what decision is made at the health centre or the provincial hospital levels, we would have an unsatisfactory outcome. I'm not sure that the issue is what to do then, I think the issue is later on. What created the dilemma is that the services which were put in there were totally unsuitable for dealing with the particular task; and what it calls for then is reorientation of the stature of the services.

It is like the story of the man who has a small battalion surrounded on all sides by the enemy. All his supply lines are cut off; he cannot have deliveries by aeroplane drop or helicopter. What does he do? I would tell him, 'Never get yourself into such a situation'. What we are being told here is that, since there is no easy or, in fact, available solution for this kind of dilemma once we get ourselves into it, the way to get ourselves out of it is by long-term planning.

I think we could broaden the fourth case slightly to include the situation that confronts the doctor in not only the poor countries. Should I go on, or should I not? Can we afford to keep the person alive? In Britain, lay groups help them make the decision as to which patient should be kept alive by artificial kidney and which should be allowed to die. In the fourth case, it is very, very difficult to decide when you have to stop; and maybe the mother has made her own decision!

Valerian P. Kimati *(Senior Officer in Paediatrics, Mwanza Hospital, Tanzania)*

Fortunately really, these sorts of extreme cases don't occur very often. Most of the babies we resuscitate do fairly well. I think it is a moral principle that we should give everybody a chance, so I would go on doing my best to treat each case according to its merits and not knowing what might happen to it tomorrow. I don't think I would compare cases of renal dialysis and their dubious results with the presented case.

As for the dilemma in the health centre, the individual has to make quick decisions on his own. The headquarters or the planning unit or his superiors cannot solve every problem, and I think most of these dilemmas should be left to the individual's common sense rather than depend on principles or rules laid down by these superiors.

Francis P. Okediji
*(Professor and Head,
Department of Sociology,
University of Ibadan,
Nigeria)*

I'm glad that medical doctors are concerned with philosophical problems. Not being a medical person, I don't have any precise answers for these dilemmas, but my suggestion is very simply that we go back to the curriculum of medical training in Africa and introduce a course in ethics, dealing with ethical problems in medical-care systems and linked to the cultural problems in African society. Once students are embarked upon this, they can take actions of their own and rationalize for such actions. I am not suggesting that the rules are there to guide in particular issues, but I think grounding in ethics of medical-care systems might help doctors when they have to face these kinds of problems and dilemmas.

Oscar Gish *(Health
Economist, Ministry of
Health, Tanzania)*

The dilemmas presented are fortunately not usually that extreme. However, they are dilemmas in the dictionary sense and I suspect that people continue to take *ad hoc* pragmatic decisions. I object to the fact that this slice of life - this dilemma - is reported to us as *fait accompli*. It does have a history and a background and as Dr Lucas indicates one must not allow oneself to be surrounded so thoroughly by the enemy.

It is important to draw the appropriate lessons from these dilemmas so that it is possible to shape the future in such a way that you don't get into these dilemmas - at least not at the extreme level that was presented. I should like to point out that the fourth dilemma only existed because it happened at a special centre with ample resources. I think it is important for us to recognize that these dilemmas are not created in any sense by the functioning health workers. They are not responsible for the situations that create these dilemmas. It is the 'decision-makers' and instructors who provide resources or don't provide the right number or quality of workers.

Unfortunately, so much of the decision-making in the health business is made by medical doctors, often representing an organized professional body unwilling to face or with no experience of the dilemmas.

Rabi Iliasu *(Principal Nursing Officer, Ministry of Health and Social Welfare, Kano State, Nigeria)*

Speaking as a nurse who has had to share responsibilities with doctors, I want to comment on the fourth case presentation in relation to our African set-up. It was well-dramatized and showed what takes place in the minds of those responsible. If I were a paediatrician, I would endeavour to continue regardless of the cost and regardless of the knowledge that this child may very likely die. This is especially so as we are trying to encourage our people to come to hospital; and despite scientific knowledge, people who hold on to a belief in God still believe that miracles do occur. We health workers, particularly on the rural level, are faced with many problems for which we have to take decisions; so, where one is faced with a number of things happening, one should treat the cases as they come regardless of what social sector they come from. Before health services are set up, one should really make plans and include those locally involved. If the village chief or district head is involved, alternative transport and facilities could very likely be produced.

Samuel Ofosu-Amaah *(Senior Lecturer in Child Health, Department of Community Health, University of Ghana Medical School, Ghana)*

My only comments are on three issues. The first is that, mercifully, in the situation in which I work I am insulated from knowing the cost of a lot of drugs that we use. Second, as a paediatrician, I just go on doing what I know I have to do, so that this is not usually a dilemma. It is a dilemma when you come to look back at what has happened. Thirdly, in our Ghanaian situation there is another merciful way out. The parents of hopelessly sick children usually will remove them from hospital. In my earlier experience I would vigorously fight this, but gradually I made more feeble attempts.

Bwembya Lukutati *(Director of Social Welfare, Ministry of Labour and Social Services, Zambia)*

I am not a medical doctor, but I think that professionals should deal with professional problems as they arise and as they feel competent. This is the individualization of dilemmas. However, some dilemmas are purely social. They call for solution within the social situation in which they occur, and ought to be thrown back to the community.

Salvator Kanani *(Assistant Director of Medical Services, Ministry of Health, Kenya)*

I was very impressed by the presentation of the dilemmas. I could see myself throughout the spheres, as I have worked in all of them; and now you might say I am planning. At that health centre, I think I would deal with the emergencies as they occurred. Having done that, I would like to find out how frequently this problem occurred in the place where I worked; having identified this problem as a number, I would like to establish a very viable system of communication with my provincial level and establish a constant source of information supply. I would, therefore, under no circumstances make that dilemma entirely mine, but have it shared between myself and those who are supposed to be above me. I also support the proposal to throw this problem back to the community in which you work.

Otikoye Ransome-Kuti *(Professor and Chairman, Department of Paediatrics, College of Medicine, University of Lagos, Nigeria)*

I have worked in paediatrics long enough to understand this problem completely. To start with I worked on the wards with a fantastic organization for diagnosis and treatment, but I found that our mortality rate was 25 to 30 per cent no matter what we did. So, I asked myself, 'What is the problem?' These babies come to the wards too late! So, we started the first emergency room in Nigeria. However, we were overrun by the enemy - we couldn't treat the children quickly enough. So, I said to myself, 'This is not the place to fight the battle'; and moved to the next university where I had to go and work in Out-patients. And there I found the same dilemma. I wasn't getting my results. At last I discovered it had to be the community. We had to tackle this problem from the roots.

What we have been shown here is a problem that you cannot solve as it was presented. A doctor just has to do what he thinks fit at a particular time. You can't even try to solve it all at once; your human energy is consumed and it is a case of either you drop dead or the next patient dies. The solution is long-term, something you have to sit down and plan patiently; and don't think developing countries should expect any dramatic results in the next five to ten years. What we have to do is put our emphasis on giving the best possible service with the resources available to us. We have to accept that, until we can move on to the next stage. The decision of what is best for each community will depend on the community detail, and will involve doctors and administrators. But, whoever administers the health services of a country must be either persons who have gone through the experience themselves or competent planners or organizers who are susceptible to advice from those who have.

Irene Thomas *(Principal Medical Officer and Head of MCH and Family Planning Programmes, Federal Ministry of Health, Nigeria)*

I started out working in an obstetrical unit, delivering babies and sometimes resuscitating them. We later established a premature unit and then an intensive-care unit. From that set-up I went into a health centre where I found that what was most important was communication with members of my staff right down to the porter and also with members of the community. I used to hold two-monthly meetings with leaders of the community, trying to get them to understand our own dilemmas in delivering health care to them, and also to understand their own dilemmas because they had plenty. I am now at the planning, decision-making stage, and it does help to have gone through the whole gamut. You don't want a repetition of the frustrations all the time. You want to deal with them, not just be complaining to the administrators or the ministry of finance. You have to go and tell them what they don't know on a level they can understand. I would say, 'Don't expect the people in the field to work miracles. You at the top must try to provide them with the resources, whether financially or technically. Give them what they should make use of, and encourage them to go on making use of what they have.'

Maaza Bekele *(Head, Social Services Department, Planning Commission, Ethiopia)*

The case is for a drastic reorganization of thinking about health services, and we have been trying to do this in Ethiopia where the service that is being offered is reaching less than 20 per cent of the people in the rural areas. That is what Ethiopia can afford; there is not the resource base for providing much more. But it is a terrible exercise because you have the people who face personal ethical dilemmas, and you have the people who face resource, planning and a higher-thinking dilemma.

How can these people work together?

An earlier speaker said, This is what you can do! Do it to the best of your ability; and try to pull all other people into it'. You have to pull people outside of the medical field into the medical problems as well. In Ethiopia medical people are working in isolation, and when we keep on hammering about getting at this problem at its roots, they think that you do this by preventive and curative work. But, unless we can do it as a community and as a whole, within our resources, the little we put into it is wasted. You get this stupid situation where a health centre is not even in the right place. It is not properly staffed. You don't have any communication between the workers in the field.

Lastly, I sympathize with the paediatricians in the last presentation, because it is children that we are dealing with. But, perhaps, in this case the mother decided for them that this was probably a waste of their human energy.

Derrick B. Jelliffe
(Professor and Head, Division of Population, Family and International Health, School of Public Health, University of California, USA)

There are two additional facets to the dilemmas faced by paediatricians. There is the dilemma of the two channels of quality, especially in the capital city; there is the private-patient hospital and the general hospital.

The dilemmas can be avoided to a limited extent by trying to streamline the techniques used in treatment so that they can be given to a person as low as possible on the skill pyramid. However, you can carry that as far as you are able and still come back for a better key to the problem. Which one are you going to treat; which one are you going to send home? I have found that one has to develop what I call a 'compassionate neglect', which is very difficult for people who have been taught to do exactly the opposite. I think the only reason why the paediatrician under these circumstances doesn't undergo some type of psychological or moral crack-up is because he has at least two protective devices. One, he doesn't have the time to reflect upon the judgements he is making all the time; and another is what I think of as a pseudo-solution, a sort of 'eye-wash' solution. We give minimal treatment to the low birth-weight baby whom we know to have very little opportunity of surviving.

He really is more or less neglected. Or, we make ward rounds and discharge a patient who has been partially treated. Because he has been treated, the Hippocratic part of our consciences is appeased; but, in fact, the child will probably go home and die.

There are two positive suggestions I would like to make. Let us avoid creating new problems. Let's hypothesize: suppose a high-powered team came to a developing country looking for chromosomal abnormalities. They would certainly find lots; and we would then be faced with the problem of what to do with them. Second, taking Dr Lucas's brilliant military analysis, we have to move from the old static faults with limited electronic field guns and resort to guerrilla warfare. We have to carry this out into the community. Although this does not help the paediatrician now, we have to see it from a long-term point of view, for we really are trapped now in totally inappropriate forms of service.

E. Ayotunde Yoloye
(Professor of Education, University of Ibadan, Nigeria)

I do agree that you first need to tackle this problem before it occurs; but, being a layman, I don't know how you do that. But, if I were faced with that sort of dilemma, I think I would have a certain set of ground rules and I would go on the basis of statistics. I would weigh the probability of either decision. The way I would reason is this: Now, if I don't do anything for this child he is certain to die. If I do something there is a chance that he might live. So I decide to do something. In the other cases, I also have a strategical position. If I don't do anything for these people who are here now, I'm pretty sure they are going to die. The epidemic may or may not occur. I'd act on the people who are here now.

If I got into a situation where I couldn't make that kind of decision, I would toss a coin!

Monica Fisher
(School Medical Officer, Ministry of Health, Zambia)

The first thing is to disagree very strongly with those who think the cases exaggerated. That fourth case history is very common indeed. Three or four have occurred in my experience just recently. We mustn't, I think, be conned into decisions which may prove later to be untrue. Babies with poor prognosis at birth have grown into healthy, productive members of the community.

I do agree that we must make use of all the other people around - not only the chief who could have a car himself, but he might know an important trader who has three. We must also make the best use of the people, themselves, in the clinic or hospital. We must bring back ethics into medicine for the whole staff, especially in a time of demarcation disputes and trade unionism. They mustn't say, 'I'm off duty. It's my coffee time.'

A.K. Joppa *(Planning Officer, Unicef)*

The dilemmas we have been shown represent particular levels or particular specialities and, if you are a doctor and have to face a dilemma, well, we have already seen the answer. You have to use your common sense. We now have to consider the dilemma at the national level, because no amount of resources put at the disposal of a particular sector, such as the health sector, will actually solve the problem. Within each sector we can only do our best with the amount we are given. The real solution to the dilemma is with the planner, the one who has to decide how to divide the national 'cake'. What are the criteria on which he bases his decisions?

I myself was faced with this kind of dilemma some time ago when I was responsible for assisting my government in deciding on the allocation of resources to the various ministries. You come to a point where you ask yourself, 'Why am I giving $20,000 to the ministry of health. Why am I not giving more?' If we want to find a solution to the whole question of the dilemma, I think we have to consider the criteria of allocation of resources between the various sectors.

Lin Chuan-chia *(Head of Child Health-Care Department, Peking Children's Hospital, People's Republic of China)*

The question, 'How are we going to do our work?' is really very important. With the lessons we have learnt through the years and as mothers, the question is very clearly vital. We heard from Tanzania at the seminar how they saw babies die of marasmus and the Nigerian representative told us how he felt when he saw pregnant women who had to walk a hundred miles on occasions for examination and delivery. And from the slides we have seen at the seminar, we have learnt how many persons are waiting for us to treat them. I have also met this question. We in China are also in a developing country and we have the same problems facing us. We have worked hard and are still working hard to solve our problems. We are making progress all the time. We can solve our problems by our own efforts and by our own hands. In spite of the difficulties, we must see the bright side of things, while we go on trying to solve the dilemma of child care.

Otikoye Ransome-Kuti   There are a few things I'd like to add because I think they are very important. Dr Jelliffe has said that we have to streamline our methods of treatment in such a way that they can be used by the least qualified manpower. I do think we should continue to do research. We don't all have to do it, but the universities and specialist units must continue to work with these methods and streamline them. We also have to collect good statistics and evaluate them, so we can then plan further research and refine our methods even further. We should not minimize the importance of this kind of work.

Jack J. Kisa *(Principal Economist, Ministry of Finance and Planning, Kenya)*   I'd like to comment on the fourth case and go back to the point made by Mr Gish that perhaps there are some lessons to be drawn from it. If one can reasonably predict the chances of survival of a child of that sort, in spite of the complications involved, and if one could somehow estimate how much it might cost to continue for any length of time to treat the child, presumably one can approach it from an economic as well as a moral point of view. Given that cost, how much could the same amount of resources, in terms of time, of personnel involved and the supplies involved, achieve in terms of saving other lives? If I can reasonably calculate that, my decision would be that I use the same resources for saving as many lives as possible and that. I think, is economically sound as well as morally sound. The concept we call 'opportunity-cost' may be higher than the actual cost, depending on the alternatives available. The dilemma is a point between two evils and you want to choose the lesser of the two. If the same amount of money is going to save ten lives, then you might as well use that for saving ten lives instead of saving only one life.

Oscar Gish

It is fairly easy for economists to utilize various cost analyses, and it may work more or less. But I don't think that these methodologies are terribly useful when you get down to the individual child. We can use these tactics and they can work in evaluating different ways of making resources available at health centre, dispensary level and so on. But it is too late once it comes to the individual child, and I am rather sympathetic to the doctor who tries to do everything possible for the individual patient who has come for treatment.

I'm sure that there are many ways in which the solution is made for us; but in practice I would be a bit afraid of the society which is so calculating that the child would be allowed to die in our faces. However, we do produce in our societies systems that allow many, many children to die, perhaps not within our view, and that is clearly a more significant dilemma. Mr Joppa pointed out the need to look at resource allocation to sectors. Yes, but after that there is the question of resource allocation within the sectors. Once it has been decided we have so much for health, we have to choose between optimal health centres, doctors, nurses and so on.

On the question of aid raised here, people give money in ways that are in keeping with their own interests, and it is also true that people ask for or take money in ways that are in their own interests. If we were more aware of the relationship, fairly technical but very important, of the capital budget to the recurrent budget, we might be more careful about the kind of aid we take. For it is the capital budget that makes tomorrow's recurrent budget, and our problems are generally with the recurrent budget.

Samuel Ofosu-Amaah

I would like to add a criticism of us doctors in our narrow-minded attitude towards resource allocation. An economist has told us that at a meeting where resources were being allocated, doctors were uninterested in discussing water or agriculture, but when hospitals were mentioned, they all sprang up to make their points.

A second point is that most of us in the medical field are unable to talk to the economists in their own language. We feel we are doing a good job; our ethical and moral services are needed. However, we have got to be brought to realize that we are competing for resources and we must learn to talk the language of whoever is going to supervise them.

Bwembya Lukutati   We are fortunate in that the group of people who actually spoil or give the last touch to our plans - the politicians - are not here. But, I would like to point out that, in considering some of the dilemmas we find professionally, whether from the medical aspect or from the economical aspect or from the social service aspect, there is a politician laughing. These dilemmas that we are in are clearly of their making. The allocation of resources to a particular region is based mainly on political grounds, and I think a lot has to be done in educating the people, who, after all, are the last to have a say in what we professionals decide.

From Perplexity to Progress: The Need to Find a Way Through

Those who work with children cannot avoid the moral dilemma, no matter how skilled or influential as planners they are. Action is demanded daily, no matter how limited the resources or how agonizing the decisions to be made. Unfortunately, the medical profession has been its own worst enemy in the struggle to make the best decisions. All too often there has been a tacit conspiracy, or trade-off, between medical specialists and planners. On the one hand, budget planners have accorded a low priority to the health programme in community terms, while, on the other, they have left the specialists largely unhindered and free to continue working within a traditional but badly structured framework, without the benefit of the carefully modelled planning that would be thought essential elsewhere. At the periphery the dilemma remains and the needs of the children remain unsatisfied.

We plan for tomorrow but, too often, for the children tomorrow never comes

Children have no vote and do not elect their own members of parliament. They are obliged to adapt to the deficient environment that envelops them and too often we see that they are forced to surrender the struggle for existence. Even the paediatricians are in an inferior position in the medical hierarchy and the parents, confronted by the relentless day-to-day struggle to exist, are unable to undergo

further sacrifices to save their children where society as a whole remains so indifferent. There is a lack of commitment to the child at every level of society and a corresponding lack of awareness of the importance of starting with the child as the take-off point in development in broad social terms. But children cannot wait for planners: the critical stage of growth comes once and once only in their lives and obliges us to examine with the utmost vigour the alternatives that are available.

The need to accept the responsibility

Management studies may help us, but in the final analysis all decisions depend on value judgements, policy decisions at the top as much as everyday operational decisions below - and no information system or analytical technique can alter this fact. Intuition and common sense are probably the basis of most decisions and although rationalization of the decision-making process may help us, it will never substitute for the value element. Yet we must start with the available resources and the need to plan. We also have a responsibility - those of us who are paediatricians - for those sick and potentially sick children who do not come to hospital; and we must acknowledge that, unless the selection of activities is carefully thought out, the end results could be 'hypertrophy of the curative, hypotrophy of the preventive and complete atrophy of the social activities'. We cannot count on adequate resources and we must not go on structuring the health programme in a manner that cannot lead to effective implementation. The unbalanced way in which health resources are now distributed has been clearly described by Gish and others. We need to stand the whole implementation structure on its head, by looking at community need first and assessing existing institutions in the light of this way of thinking. All levels of service are still needed, for the health worker will always have need to make the specialized service available to the sick mother and child. But medicine must be planned to serve people and not the interests of doctors.

Gaining the maximum impact

It is true that the generalization of health resources would not by itself lead to much progress. If limited resources were redistributed to cover the whole country it might be possible to reach everybody, yet the spread would be so thin and the resulting quality of service so low that no one would benefit. We must therefore find the breakthrough point on the cost/distribution curve at which we can achieve the maximum impact. Planning tools are available and we need to overcome our fear of using them. We must also not be afraid to step outside the traditional limits of the profession: we must establish a continuous dialogue with those working in economics, sociology, public administration, agriculture, social welfare and education if we are to make the right decisions. This is a challenge both to doctors and to conventional planners: health service planning has been bedevilled for too long by a reluctance by all concerned to step outside their professional boundaries.

The gulf between the top and the bottom

There is a vast distance between the planner at the top of the (so-called) pyramid and the health worker in the field expected to interpret decisions. In the situations that confront the health practitioner, problems that can be neatly categorized as 'clinical', 'biomedical', 'social' or 'economic' do not exist. Real problems do not have interdisciplinary boundaries - they are simply interpreted in different ways. While the planner at the centre may give priority to preventive measures and insist on their implementation, the health worker in the field may be overwhelmed by immediate demands for treatment. Paediatricians working in the African countries face broadly the same problems in the background and development of the health services, for the epidemiology of the African child is monotonously uniform. Least privileged among the underprivileged, receiving only a limited share of limited resources, African children generally face a life of misery.

Start with the needs of the child

The health programme must be determined by the needs of the child. We have seen that the satisfaction of these needs is of special importance in the early development of the child, both as an individual and as the basic unit, in microcosm, of society. It is the experience of many governments, as a British Health Minister recently declared, that there will never be a country that has enough resources to meet all the demands that will be made on the nation's health service. But we must succeed in setting the child as our priority. This is especially so in less developed countries, as can be seen

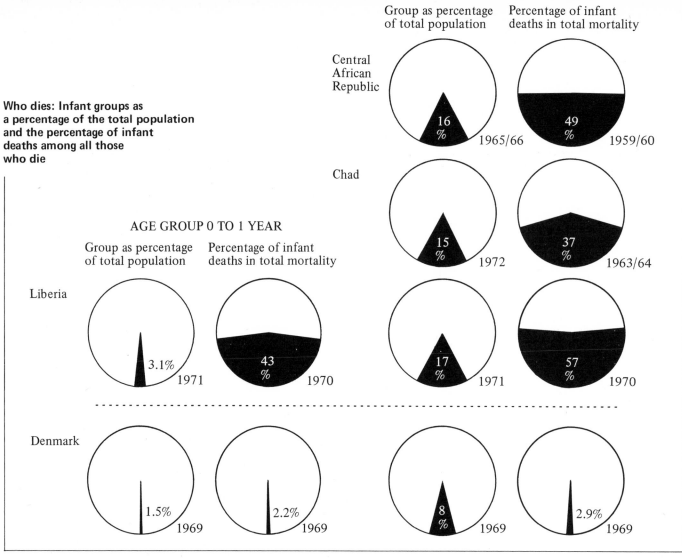

Who dies: Infant groups as a percentage of the total population and the percentage of infant deaths among all those who die

AGE GROUP 0 TO 4 YEARS

Group as percentage of total population

Percentage of infant deaths in total mortality

Central African Republic

16 % — 1965/66

49 % — 1959/60

Chad

15 % — 1972

37 % — 1963/64

17 % — 1971

57 % — 1970

AGE GROUP 0 TO 1 YEAR

Group as percentage of total population

Percentage of infant deaths in total mortality

Liberia

3.1% — 1971

43 % — 1970

Denmark

1.5% — 1969

2.2% — 1969

8 % — 1969

2.9% — 1969

124

from a study of national death profiles and age distribution of these societies (see the diagram on page 124).

Must the children die? Infant mortality rates - deaths among children below the age of 1 - in Africa range for varying periods from 80 to over 200 per 1,000 live births, with an average for twenty-three subSaharan countries of 150. (For comparison figures for 1973 for some industrialized countries are as follows: Australia (1972) 16.7, Canada 16.8, Denmark (1971) 13.5, Japan 11.7, Soviet Union 26.3, Sweden 9.6, United States of America 17.6.) The available figures, for Africa, conceal the true extent of the problem, deriving as they do for the most part from inadequate sample surveys sometimes drawn from urban areas and under-recording often by considerable margins. A study of the United Nations *Demographic Yearbook* reveals that vital statistics for Africa are the least reliable in the world and this in itself is a reflection of overall poverty in that the cost of accurate registration and survey is beyond the resources of most of these poor territories. But the general pattern is perfectly clear: it is that of preponderant infant mortality, largely among the rural masses, which are in many cases cut off from any medical help whatsoever.

Less research, more action The solution to the problem of infant mortality and child care as a whole will make possible the remodelling of the total health structure, in medical and social terms, along the lines necessary to meet basic health needs in the rural context. This is because so many other dimensions to the problem must be taken into account for its solution. The narrowly medical components of the programme will not be sufficient in themselves. There is now fairly broad agreement on what all the inputs should be. Further research may add precision to the tools of analysis but without back-up finance these will not contribute much to the short-term future. The priority is for action now, on the basis of less-expensive intellectual technology that is concerned with what is feasible in present conditions, and not with all-embracing targets where these cannot be realized through the limited budgets of African

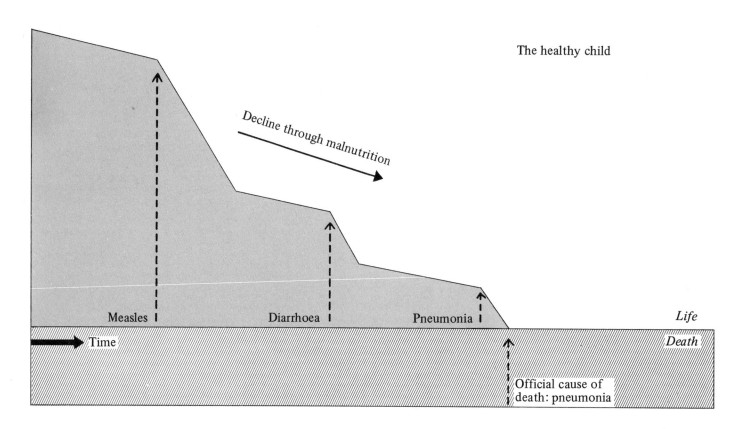

The healthy child

Decline through malnutrition

Measles | Diarrhoea | Pneumonia | *Life*

Time   *Death*

Official cause of
death: pneumonia

What killed the child?

countries. For this purpose we need to study carefully the concrete situation to see how best the package - the totality of components - can be designed, and to re-examine the role of international and national agencies to see where their activities, though well-intentioned, represent the under-utilization or duplication of valuable distribution networks or campaigns that would be better harnessed to integrated, multiple-delivery efforts.

Needs and wants: starting with the people

The distinction should be drawn between health needs and health demands. The satisfaction of needs concerns, essentially, the health programme as designed from above, in terms of control or eradication measures conceived at the national level; it may not correspond to the true demand since this itself is not fully expressed. Access to service is often poor, for a variety of reasons: absence of transport, lack of awareness of health rights (stemming from inadequate education and lack of a sense of local or national identity), resistance of local despots to 'interference' from outside. The programme should therefore begin with the point of delivery and the point of maximum need - in Africa this must be the rural areas - and with the idea of training local people to deliver the package.

Not the pyramid, but the broad front

Nothing is to be gained by the removal to the cities, for training, of motivated local people - for indefinite periods - to swell the numbers of urban dispossessed and to begin the climb of elitism up a ladder that leads to brain drain or disillusionment. Resources are not adequate to provide a full 'professional' service on a mobile basis: it is better therefore to promote the local service and the local auxiliary to health worker (starts have already been made in this direction in a number of countries). At the local level the ethical conflicts that we have examined will be resolved in ways that are not open to the traditional physician tied to the Hippocratic oath. The latter is not 'free' to devote his trained time, for example, to showing local people through the microscope the parasites swarming in village water - as a Chinese doctor did - in order first to establish the priority of environmental hygiene. In some ways, the physician-centred health-care system is positively counter-productive, and doubly so in the less-developed countries that are not able to back up the 'professional' system by substantial resources. Reform is called for in medical structures and this needs to be buttressed by re-establishing the authority of local people and their right - and the importance of the right - to minister to themselves. In some remote parts of Africa still without schools, doctors or clinics people are none the less able to buy Coca-Cola, for example, without difficulty and it might well be that a non-monetary 'tax' on commercial enterprises would be the obligation to make distribution facilities available for the needs of health and other programmes where no other transport is at present available. The development of community concern will be necessary in order to provide the back-up support for good sanitation, adequate and drinkable water, reliable transport and information lines and local education drives, all of which are essential to the viability of the health-care programme.

Half a loaf is better than none: setting the intermediate target

The key idea in the child-care programme must be that of achieving intermediate goals. In a sense, these are the only goals when other goals are unattainable, and the word 'intermediate' gives a poor idea of the value to be derived from the achievement of any target in the short term. We need to prove that a limited target may be set - and reached - in order to break through the deadlock and generate greater confidence. The key to the achievement of intermediate goals must itself lie in coming to grips with infant mortality. Success in this area will do more than in any other to strengthen the morale of the community and to support the case for intermediate technology, for it can yield results that are much more easily understood and related to the investment of effort (than, for example, degrees of malnutrition). Mastering the problem of infant mortality requires the concerted intervention of medical inputs designed in relation to what is feasible in a planned reduction of mortality, and delivered through the child-care package.

The Child Care Package

	Pregnancy	Birth		
Social inputs	Preparation of parents for childhood	Family welfare / Child spacing		Socialization
Perinatal care		7 days		
Nutrition				2 to 3 years
Immunization		1 year		
Hygiene and environmental sanitation				

The child-care package: a critical time

The Package Programme

The aim of the package programme is to try to make available an integrated programme of child health care that will be suitable for contexts where service at present does not exist, because of limited resources, or in which the result of present expenditures is not satisfactory because of lack of coordination of effort, unbalanced distribution of health investments, and other factors that represent, taken as a whole, a failure to recognize the importance of the integrated approach.

The components of the package may be classified in terms of medico-social inputs, 'hardware' (manuals, weight-chart cards, teaching aids, etc.) and implementation in human terms, i.e. answering the question of who will deliver the package and to whom.

There is a tendency to exaggerate the importance of the physical aids; the existence of medical 'kits' for the package purpose may serve well to dramatize the idea of the integrated package, but not if there is no back-up in personnel capable of using these tools and if their misuse or waste is going to be counterproductive socially and financially. The overpromotion of such aids may reflect an unhealthy reliance on western technology at the expense of local development, particularly in the dependence on imported products rather than on the efforts of local people.

The human element in implementation is of fundamental importance. Planning has to provide for appropriate staffing to implement the programme, which will otherwise remain at the drawing-board stage, unrealized. Such staff need to be recruited, trained, employed and supported in their own locality. Those concerned with the delivery of services need to broaden their horizons and acquire or know how to utilize expertise from any useful and valid quarter within or outside their own speciality. With these points in mind, a number of elements were proposed for the optimum package of integrated child care: (1) the social inputs (preparation of parents for parenthood, family welfare and child-spacing; the socialization process); (2) perinatal care; (3) nutrition in infancy and childhood; (4) immunization and related measures; (5) hygiene and environmental sanitation.

The treatment of diseases after they have been contracted, i.e. conventional curative medicine in the hospital-oriented setting, lies outside the scope of the largely preventive measures of the child-care package considered here, even though it will continue to be a permanent necessity within the total health picture. Curative medicine is, in any case, already receiving a major share of health resources, and by thus absorbing a preponderant part of the health budget it contributes indirectly to the continual postponement of preventive measures. It should be noted however, that though seldom highly cost-effective, it may have considerable impact - in the use of antibiotics against pneumonia, for example.

Properly conceived and executed, an effective programme of health and welfare for children must begin with the family and the family situation. The parents must be adequately prepared to receive and take care of the child when born and this implies good physical and mental health, some source of regular income to sustain the family, and a basic minimum of education and information in order to understand and plan for children both before and after childbirth.

A family that is adequately prepared for parenthood is one that is also aware of the importance of the other elements in the package; a well-informed community will make its needs known and will support the services required. This is not yet generally the case in Africa: the level of education and literacy is low; the economic base is shallow; and facilities for welfare and other services are largely non-existent. It is therefore necessary to design the package of health and social inputs in such a way as to maximize the return on investment in terms of human priorities and scarcity of resources.

Human vulnerability is at its greatest around childbirth and this is reflected in the construction of the package, the elements of which are largely concerned with the perinatal and postperinatal periods. The interdisciplinary effort called for in the design of the optimum package will include economic evaluation, and the sections in this part are therefore preceded by a brief glossary of economic formulations that may be useful to those health workers who are not familiar with economics. This is followed by a paper on the degree of preventiveness in infant mortality.

The conventional attack on large-scale problems in the health field is based on the identification of specific health needs, in part through the registration of statistics on mortality and morbidity. This method of data collection requires a considerable investment of resources in the recruitment of regional registrars and the collation of statistics over long periods (largely from death certificates, where these exist) and often does little more than confirm the generally suspected epidemiological pattern, without offering new solutions to actual problems. In the paper on preventiveness, an alternative approach is outlined that is not only based on the examination of data - in this case from existing hospital records - but that is also intended to provide one method of achieving better results in remedial treatment by means of an initial classification of infant mortality groups according to specific factors that identify

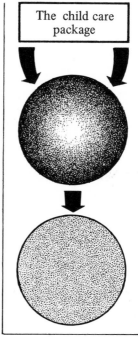

The child care
package

Urban
adult

The rural
child

High *Health inputs* Low

**The child care package
means equal distribution
of resources**

varying degrees of preventiveness. Once these groups are identified, phased improvements may be aimed at that are related to what is actually feasible in given circumstances.

The three studies in cost-effectiveness that follow were constructed to illustrate the similar impact that could be made upon infant mortality through perinatal care, nutrition and immunization, by programmes written in terms of the more specific identification of problems in relation to cost, again to try to pinpoint more narrowly the scope for practical improvement. These studies were based, for comparability, upon a hypothetical African country of 10 million population with the following features: (a) relatively low population density, with some 10 to 15 per cent of the population in urban areas and 85 to 90 per cent in rural areas; (b) population growth around 2.5 to 3 per cent, with a birth rate of 50/1,000 and an infant mortality rate of 150/1,000; (c) 20 per cent of the population under 6 years of age and almost 50 per cent under 15 years of age; (d) *per capita* income US$100 to US$150; (e) ministry of health budget equal to US$2 per capita; (f) one-third to two-thirds of registered doctors in the metropolis.

Such a national pattern clearly does no more than give a general indication of the working context and particular country contexts would produce different patterns in similar studies. It is hoped, however, that the presentation of such exercises will promote their emulation in specific national situations. The three studies each present an inevitably simplified one-dimensional picture. The main criteria used are reduction of mortality and cost per life saved and it has to be accepted that a measurement of human life in money terms, even negatively, is not only invidious but also difficult to carry out. None the less, the notoriously high mortality rates in infancy and childhood in developing countries indicate that reduction of mortality must be the prime objective of any health programme and this must be the justification, if justification there need be, for the concentration on death itself.

After the background papers had been delivered and after the presentation of the dilemmas and the three studies in cost-effectiveness, the seminar divided into working groups to consider the component elements of the package and their observations are printed here together with editorial commentary. This part is concluded by a section that is intended to sum up the methods of cross-evaluating the component elements of the package and to consider the approaches to delivery, essentially the question of personnel.

Means to Implementation

Some Terms of Economic Analysis

Perhaps the best-known implements for resource-related evaluation are *cost-benefit* analysis and *cost-effectiveness* analysis. When different options are feasible an evaluation has to be made by comparing the advantages and disadvantages of each alternative and for such evaluation economists often use cost-benefit and cost-effectiveness analysis, both of which measure input in the same way, that is, in monetary terms. The difference is in the measurement of output. Cost-benefit analysis tries to value *all* socially relevant outcomes, usually in monetary terms, e.g. cost of external effects (see below) of having a disease; cost of a life saved; cost of production losses, etc.; and conversely the benefits of treating a disease; the benefit of a life saved to the individual as well as to society; production benefits, etc. Cost-effectiveness analysis on the other hand concentrates on one major outcome, such as number of deaths prevented, without necessarily valuing it in terms of money.

More specifically, these forms of analysis may be defined as follows:

Cost-benefit analysis: The systematic comparison - in monetary terms - of all the costs and benefits of proposed alternative schemes with a view to determining: (a) which scheme or combination of schemes will contribute most to the achievement of predetermined objectives *at a fixed investment;* or (b) the magnitude of the benefit that can result from schemes requiring *the minimum investment.*

The resources required per unit of benefit must be determined, account being taken of the fact that costs and benefits accrue with time. (WHO.[*])

Cost-effectiveness analysis: A procedure used when benefits are difficult to measure or when those that are measurable are not commensurable. It is similar to cost-benefit analysis except that benefit, instead of being expressed in monetary terms, is expressed in terms of results achieved, e.g. number of lives saved or number of days free from disease. (WHO.[*])

Cost-effectiveness measurement is a method of comparing the costs of achieving an agreed object in different ways (G & R[*]). It is a modified form of cost-benefit analysis which is used when costs and benefits are difficult to measure or to express in units that are commensurate. The aim of cost-effectiveness analysis is *to determine the cheapest means of achieving a given objective or to obtain the maximum value for a specified expenditure. (S.[*])*

The following are some other useful economic terms:

Effectiveness: The ratio between the achievement of the programme activity and the desired level which, during the planning process, the planners had proposed would result from the programme activity. (WHO.[*])

Efficiency: The ratio between the result that might be achieved through the expenditure of a specified amount of resources and the result that might be achieved through a minimum of expenditure. (WHO.[*])

External effects (Externalities) are the costs and benefits which were not included in the budget and are additional to the direct operating costs and benefits. They are mainly the social consequences of projects and must be taken into account to be able to appraise the social optimality of a project. (S.[*])

Health demands are usually measures in terms of the utilization of health services. Consideration must be given to the fact that all felt needs by a population (most usually in curative medicine) cannot be translated into expressed need or demand for various reasons (absence of accessible health services, lack of information, lack of confidence, low income, etc.). (WHO.[*])

Health needs may be defined as scientifically (biologically, epidemiologically, etc.) determined deficiencies in health that call for preventive, curative and eventually control or eradication measures. (WHO.[*])

Marginal cost analysis: A procedure where the increase in total cost which results from the production of an additional unit of output is calculated.

Overstatement: If a person has two or more diseases simultaneously, eliminating one still leaves him with one or more diseases, which may also contribute to disability, premature death or continued expenditures for medical treatment. When treatment and prognosis differ, the benefits calculated for one disease at a time constitute an overstatement. The extent of overstatement is affected by the degree of interdependence in the origin of diseases, so that individuals and families with multiple problems present the greatest potential for overstatement. In general, it is worth emphasizing that the presence of multiple diseases and of competing causes of death means that the total benefits of eliminating or controlling several diseases cannot be arrived at by summing the calculated economic benefits of individual programmes. (K.[*])

[*]G & R: Grundy & Reinke, 1973; K: Klarman, 1965; S: Seccombe, 1970; WHO: World Health Organization, 1973

Degree of Preventiveness in Infant Mortality

This study was prepared by Göran Sterky

Degree of preventiveness may be defined by the extent to which the therapeutic activity alters favourably the natural course of disease, by its eradication, for example, through specific vaccination or early treatment (Hutchison, 1960). It can also be expressed as an index of vulnerability, i.e. the prospect of preventing mortality in terms of present knowledge and methods. The criterion of vulnerability should form part of any analysis of the death rate undertaken in connexion with planning. There are still insufficient data available for any kind of precise expression of this concept in quantitative terms and it remains a field with ample scope for future research.

Infant mortality rate is one of the most widely used measurements to determine the level of development in a nation or in a community. It is certainly not a new yardstick, and it has been a weapon for those arguing for social development and quality in health care for over one hundred years. Most of the countries now called developed had an infant mortality rate at the turn of the century equivalent to that of developing countries today (see figure 1).

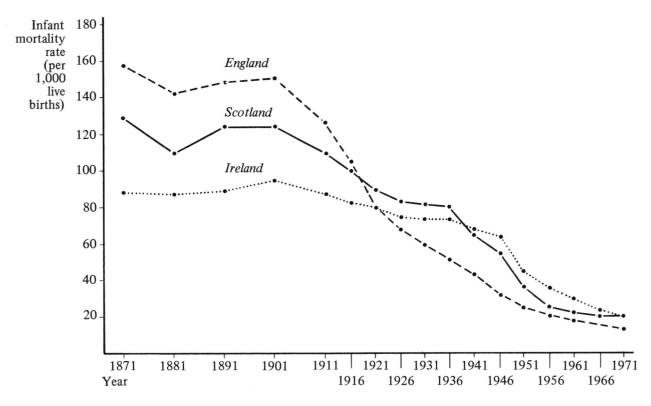

Figure 1   Comparison of infant mortality rates in England, Scotland and Ireland, 1871-1970 (Aykroyd & Kevany, 1973)

Could something relevant to the present situation in developing countries be learnt from the cause of the decline in infant mortality elsewhere? This question has recently been dealt with by Aykroyd & Kevany (1973), who conclude: 'Experience in developed countries shows that what is specially needed to remedy the situation is improvement in domestic sanitation, cleaner water supplies, the extension of maternity and child welfare services, and the satisfactory feeding of infants.' It has not been possible to single out a predominant factor; the downward trend in infant mortality rates, which began quite suddenly at the beginning of this century, was due to a combination of factors influencing many aspects of human life.

Can health services contribute towards bringing about such a change in the developing countries? If so, to what degree? What are realistic stage-by-stage objectives that each country should set? One of the basic principles of planning is that the aims of a programme must meet the condition of feasibility. The feasibility of an objective largely depends on the point of departure. If, for example, the infant mortality rate in a given place is 100 per 1,000 live births, there will be little possibility of lowering the rate to 10 within a lifetime, regardless of resources available to reduce it.

Is an infant mortality rate of 100 high or low? The answer requires the establishment of a suitable standard of comparison. The rating of a situation as satisfactory will depend on what may be attainable in the circumstances. In one set of guidelines for health planning we have the following suggestion: 'A comparison will have to be made between the result that would be obtained in terms of mortality and morbidity if the resources were allocated in a different manner, if they were employed at full capacity, and if inefficient techniques were replaced' (CENDES, 1965).

Two efforts to move along these lines may be given here. Both are drawn from the Ethiopian scene, the first from Tayback & Prince (1965) and the second by the author. The first required ten observers (registrars), staying in different localities of the Ethiopian plateau for a period of twelve months, and represented a standard approach. The second required the examination and analysis of one set of existing infant-mortality records drawn from an Addis Ababa children's clinic, and represents an attempt to describe intermediate targets.

Vital events registration: a standard approach

In 1964-65 Tayback & Prince conducted a birth and infant death registration project in five small towns considered to be reasonably representative of the population of the Ethiopian highland plateau. The method employed was that of vital events registration based on continuous observation. The life-table technique was found to be uniquely suited to capture all available information (table 1). The final value in the last column, i.e. 0.848, describes the proportion of infants born alive who will manage to survive one full year. Given in the usual terms by which infant mortality rates are stated, this can be written as 152 infant deaths per 1,000 live births. It was observed that 59 per cent of the total loss of lives took place during the first two months of infancy and that the remainder of the deaths were fairly evenly distributed over the remaining ten months. The authors believed 'that careful attention to these data can suggest the strategy for reducing the preventable segments of this heavy loss of life during infancy'. In 43 of the 75 deaths it was possible to determine with reasonable accuracy the cause of death. Taking the 32 unknown causes of deaths and 11 premature births as not preventable, it would be possible to reduce the infant mortality to 88 per 1,000.

To accomplish such a reduction a five-point programme is proposed: (a) each delivery to be attended by a community nurse; (b) each infant born alive to be visited by the community nurse by the third day; (c) each mother of a newborn to be provided with a bassinet; (d) each infant to be visited bi-weekly by the community nurse until 8 weeks old; (e) each infant to be seen in clinic or at home by the community nurse bi-monthly until 1 year of age. The manpower requirement to cover the country would be at least 4,000 community nurses, occupied full-time in MCH care.

Table 1
Consolidated life table for infants born in five towns in Ethiopia (from Tayback & Prince, 1965)

Age in months	Infant month experience	Number of deaths	Probability of dying	Probability of surviving to stated period
0 to 1	647	47	0.073	1.000
1 to 2	558	10	0.018	0.927
2 to 3	496	6	0.012	0.910
3 to 4	429	3	0.007	0.899
4 to 5	367	2	0.005	0.893
5 to 6	311	1	0.003	0.889
6 to 7	261	2	0.008	0.886
7 to 8	209	1	0.005	0.879
8 to 9	148	1	0.007	0.875
9 to 12	242*	2	0.024	0.869
12 on				0.848

Sum of: 118 infant months experience, 9 to 10 months of age; 80 infant months, 10 to 11 months of age; and 44 infant months experience, 11 to 12 months of age.

Intermediate targets:
An approach through
degrees of preventiveness

All records of infants admitted to the Ethio-Swedish Paediatric Clinic during the period 1969-72 and dying within the first 12 months of life were retrospectively scrutinized by the author. Almost all records contained a social and medical history of sufficient comprehensiveness to provide such information as when the infant was taken ill, whether the mother had received antenatal care, the place of delivery, what kind of treatment had been given prior to admission, etc. This information was then utilized to assign each infant death to one of four classes, using criteria that are given below. There were very few diagnoses of infants that could not be classified according to one of the class groups, but it should be stressed, however, that the same classification would probably not be possible in other age groups with different types of prevalent diagnoses.

The four classes of preventiveness were defined as follows:

I. *Lack of prevention in spite of the existence of available resources.* The treatment of the child had been delayed, inadequate or wrong owing to avoidable inefficiency at authorized health clinics.
II. *Inadequate health consciousness among parents, leading to late arrival or lack of utilization of available services.* Treatment often delayed by consultation with indigenous practitioners. Conditions definitely treatable in the capital.
III. *Lack of resources on the part of health authorities.* Parents consulted clinics or hospitals, but conditions were unpreventable and untreatable in the capital at present, though treatable at centres in developed countries.
IV. *Nothing but palliative treatment available anywhere or conditions not preventable at all.*

As almost all deaths of low-birth-weight infants delivered in hospitals or clinics were assigned to Class III, there are too few deaths in Class IV. The distribution among classes was rather similar in 1970-72, but in 1969 there was a higher percentage in

Class II. This may be interpreted as parental health knowledge having improved over the ensuing years.

The result of the analysis is shown in table 2. There were 378 deaths (49.7 per cent) during the first month, 71 (9.4 per cent) during the second month and 20 to 40 during each one of the following months. The distribution between each class and month as calculated in percentage of the total number (760 cases) is illustrated in figure 2. The distribution for the first month, carried out separately, is shown in figure 3. As seen in figure 2, the cumulative curve is not smooth, owing to an unexpected peak in the 7th month. This curve, analysed by semi-logarithmic plotting of the data, is seen to be due to an increase in the number of deaths in Classes III and IV. The number of cases is not that many (table 2) and an investigation of the causes of death in month 7 showed no distinguishable difference from that in months 6 or 8. The total curve was quite smooth in semi-logarithmic plotting.

To be able to extrapolate from these observations about the distribution of infant deaths at the Ethio-Swedish Paediatric Clinic and to extend these to the population of Addis Ababa the following assumptions were made: (a) the distribution of causes of death in the various classes is similar at the paediatric clinic to that throughout the rest of the capital; (b) the distribution of infants' deaths among various age groups is similar at the paediatric clinic to that throughout the capital. These assumptions may be supported by the very similar percentage of deaths in the various months in the material from the Ethio-Swedish Paediatric Clinic to that of the wider community material collected by Tayback & Prince. Preliminary data from a study of a district within Addis Ababa also give the same age distribution (Kidane et al., 1975). The pattern of morbidity at the paediatric clinic is also very similar to that in MCH clinics in the capital (Freij et al., 1973).

Table 2
Degree of preventiveness
(number of cases) in infant
mortality as analysed from
hospital material over a
four-year period

Age group	Class of preventiveness				Total
	I	II	III	IV	
0 - 1 (weeks)	10	55	85	31	181
1 - 2	32	22	35	13	102
2 - 3	16	14	17	3	50
3 - 4	10	14	14	7	45
1 - 2 (months)	15	25	23	8	71
2 - 3	11	21	3	4	39
3 - 4	7	22	4	2	35
4 - 5	13	16	6	3	38
5 - 6	10	21	3	1	35
6 - 7	10	24	6	2	42
7 - 8	10	19	2	1	32
8 - 9	13	10	1	0	24
9 - 10	7	11	6	1	25
10 - 11	12	7	0	1	20
11 - 12	8	6	4	3	21
Total	184	287	209	80	760

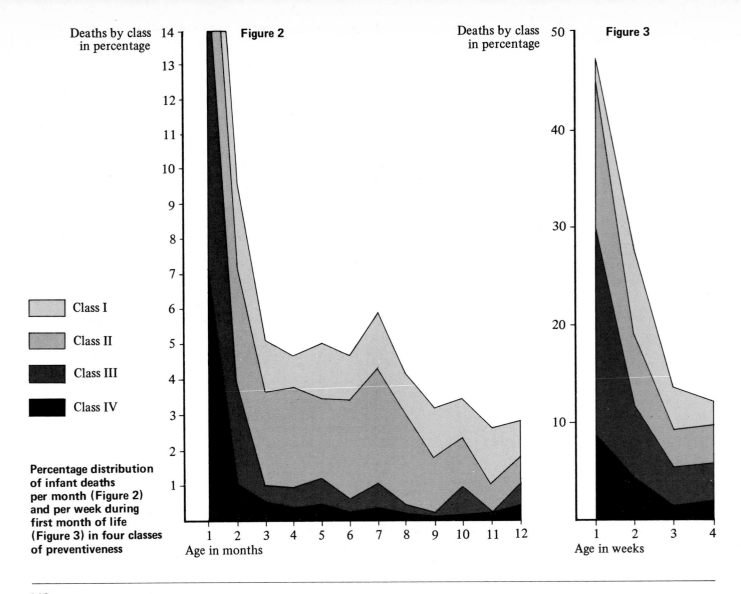

Deaths by class in percentage

Figure 2

Class I

Class II

Class III

Class IV

Age in months

Deaths by class in percentage

Figure 3

Age in weeks

Percentage distribution of infant deaths per month (Figure 2) and per week during first month of life (Figure 3) in four classes of preventiveness

From a population survey in Addis Ababa in 1967 the following projections were utilized:

1. The population of Addis Ababa in the year 1973 is 1 million.
2. The crude birth rate is 43 per 1,000.
3. The infant mortality rate is 165/175 per 1,000 live births but assumed to decline. A figure of 160 was thus used.

Combining these figures for Addis Ababa with those from the Ethio-Swedish Paediatric Clinic (table 2) the expected numbers per year would be:

1. Out of 43,000 births, 6,880 deaths will occur.
2. During the first month 3,420 deaths will occur.
3. Infant deaths distributed in classes would be:

Class	I	II	III	IV	Total
Number	1,667	2,591	1,892	729	6,880
Percentage	24.2	37.7	27.5	10.6	100.0

4. Infant mortality rate in the four classes would be:

Class	I	II	III	IV	Total
Per thousand	38.7	60.3	44.0	17.0	160.0
Cumulative rate per thousand	160.0	121.3	61.0	17.0	

If the cumulative figures are combined with the classification of preventiveness the following interpretation could be offered:

1. The infant mortality could be reduced immediately with little extra cost and

effort from 160 to 121 (class I preventiveness) with proper utilization of available health service.

2. Health service, health education and environmental hygiene could bring the mortality down to 61 per thousand.

3. Further reduction to 17 per thousand will not be feasible until a major change of socio-economic background factors takes place and a fairly expensive health service is made available.

The type of analysis described here makes use of data that are already available and thus is not prohibitively expensive to carry out. It would be feasible in any community where health data have been gathered. The results would help in establishing realistic objectives adapted to local conditions.

Conclusion

The approach represented by the Tayback & Prince study is the traditional method; it has been utilized more recently in the Inter-American investigation of mortality in childhood (Puffer & Serrano, 1973). After the monitoring of birth and infant death registration has been completed and plotted against infant age, the mortality pattern is revealed, exposing those areas in the pattern that would most likely repay the concentration of resource effort in their direction. Alas, the minimum staffing requirement, posited by Tayback & Prince in 1965, to accomplish a reduction of infant mortality to 88 per 1,000 as a follow-up to the analysis is so unlikely a target as to give the exercise a purely theoretic value. We realize how remote is the 1965 target of 5,000 full-time community nurses when we know that as late as 1973 there were still only 300 such nurses in the whole of Ethiopia.

The approach to preventiveness through the attempt to identify those infant-mortality groups that would repay particular attention represents an effort to be more specific in contributing to the preparation of health programmes that are backed by severely limited resources. That proper utilization of available health service would alone achieve an improvement of 38 per 1,000 suggests that consideration should be given first to this problem. Identification of the different breakthrough levels by class of preventiveness would enable the medical planner to achieve intermediate goals that, even if modest, would none the less be feasible. In addition, the analysis of existing hospital mortality records for degree-of-preventiveness classification is likewise feasible, and does not require the investiture of time and specialized manpower called for by birth and infant-death surveys that, moreover, do not supply data which in practice can be used for intermediate targets.

Three Studies in Cost-Effectiveness

Perinatal Care

Prepared in
collaboration with
Nebiat Tafari

The perinatal period is defined as the period extending between the 28th week of pregnancy and the 7th day of life. Death of the unborn child (the foetus) and the newly born infant during this period constitutes perinatal mortality. Death of foetus can occur before the onset of labour *(prepartum)*, during labour *(intrapartum)* or during the first 7 days of life (early neonatal death). Death of the pregnant woman from pregnancy or childbirth constitutes maternal mortality.

Death of the foetus before the onset of labour is believed to be the result of unfavourable uterine environment. Some babies are expelled from the uterus before the normal period of pregnancy has elapsed; others are born at the right time but show retardation in their growth. Some are infected and others malformed. Whatever the process that produces these abnormalities in foetuses also kills them.

Foetal death during labour is the direct result of difficulties, primarily mechanical, in expelling or extracting the foetus from the uterus. These difficulties can also kill the mother.

Live-born babies that result from an unfavourable uterine environment run a high risk of dying during the immediate postnatal period. Nearly half of the early neonatal deaths occur during the first day of life. Most of these deaths are due to failure to establish normal breathing, usually secondary to asphyxia (death by suffocation). Most deaths occur in premature babies that are born either before the term of pregnancy is completed (pre-term babies) or in babies that failed to grow normally for the length of pregnancy (small-for-dates). The remaining half of the deaths during the first week of life can be attributed to complications of abnormalities in the uterine environment and the birth process. Among leading causes of death are infections prior to delivery, respiratory failures as a result of immature lungs (e.g. hyaline membrane disease), aspiration pneumonias (equivalent to drowning in an infected pool) and birth injury. Modern neonatal care has reduced mortality from these complications but a large number of babies continue to die, even in industrialized countries.

It is apparent from the foregoing that the source of perinatal and maternal mortality is the pregnancy itself. Therefore, the identification of high-risk pregnancy leading to excessive perinatal and maternal mortality would be an important step in prevention.

Thanks to advances in obstetrics, a large number of high-risk pregnancies can be identified by simple examinations. For the purposes of prevention of perinatal mortality, surveillance during pregnancy can start between the 20th and 26th week of gestation, with the second examination between the 32nd and 34th week and the third in the 36th week. These examinations will establish: (a) the general state of health of the pregnant woman; (b) history of previous obstetric catastrophes, as these would increase the risk of death of the present foetus, whatever the cause; (c) growth of the foetus as judged by weight gain during pregnancy and/or increase in the size of the uterus; (d) the presence of infection: generalized (e.g. syphilis) or localized (e.g. pyelonephritis); (e) abnormal presentation (i.e. position of foetus in the womb) and foeto-pelvic disproportion that could cause obstructed labour; (f) prepartum haemorrhage; (g) pre-eclampsia (a specific obstetric abnormality characterized by hypertension, protein in urine and excessive weight gain or oedema).

High-risk pregnancy always results in high-risk infant, unless shown otherwise. Thus such expectant mothers must be kept under especially close surveillance and the high-risk infants that result from such pregnancies must be closely supervised in an observation unit so that well-timed, skilled obstetric and infant care can be given.

Since perinatal and maternal deaths result from abnormalities in pregnancy, emphasis must be laid on obstetric care. This is even more important in less-developed countries with deficient existing establishments in obstetric care and limited resources for future development in this area. In no other field of medicine is there a greater need for equal distribution of services to meet the need of the entire stratum of the population than in perinatal care, since high perinatal mortality and maternal death are closely related to the socio-economic status of the expectant mother.

The study

The hypothetical developing country has a population of 10 million and a birth rate of 50/1,000 population, yielding 500,000 deliveries. In the process of childbirth at least 46,400 lives would be lost: 38,400 foetuses and 8,000 mothers. The breakdown of foetal death reveals that over 60 per cent of the deaths occur before the foetus is delivered. One in every five foetuses dies during the process of delivery. (It is believed that the majority of maternal deaths occur also during this time, usually as a result of obstructed labour.) Tafari & Ross (1973) have described the dramatic results to be achieved in a less-developed country by special perinatal care for high-risk pregnancies.

Table 3

Estimated perinatal and maternal mortality in a country of 10 million population with a birth rate of 50/1,000 of population

Total deliveries		*500,000*
Perinatal death		38,400
Prepartum	16,000	
Intrapartum	8,800	
Early neonatal	13,600	
Maternal death		8,000
Total		46,400

From table 3, it can be seen that pregnancy and childbirth are more dangerous to the foetus than to the mother. Measures taken to reduce foetal loss would automatically reduce maternal death. However, additional arrangements are required to save the lives of newly borns at risk (about 10 per cent of all live-born infants) by assisting them in the difficult period of extra-uterine adaptation. About 1.5 per cent of all live-born infants would require hospitalization in a special-care unit because of very low birth weight (less than 2 kg) or continued sickness.

'Standard' perinatal care (hereafter called 'standard'care). Hospital-based perinatal practice in which the following care is given:
    'Standard' Programme A: Three antenatal visits and hospital delivery for 80 per cent of all expectant mothers.
    'Standard' Programme B: Programme A plus observation unit for high-risk newborns.
    'Standard' Programme C: Programme A plus Programme B plus special-care unit for low-birth-weight and sick newborns.

Maternity village perinatal care (hereafter called 'village' care). Rural-health-centre-based perinatal practice for expectant mothers in which the following are given:

'Village' Programme A: Surveillance of 80 per cent of all expectant mothers by peripheral health workers with a deliberate attempt at selection of high-risk pregnancies. Three antenatal visits resulting in identification of high-risk pregnancies. Because of transport difficulties, these mothers need to be accommodated in a 'maternity village' well before the onset of labour (at 36 to 38 weeks of pregnancy) with delivery of these mothers in hospitals or clinics with specially trained staff. It is estimated that 10 per cent of all pregnancies are high-risk.

'Village' Programme B: Programme A plus observation unit for high-risk infants.

'Village' Programme C: Programme A plus Programme B plus special-care unit for low-birth-weight and sick newborns.

Prevention of death as the result of the proposed solutions. The following results may be calculated from the programmes:

'Standard' care (table 4). As a result of Programme A, the number of perinatal infant deaths is reduced by over 30 per cent with 75 per cent reduction in maternal mortality. The introduction of Programme B would further reduce foetal deaths by 14 per cent while Programme C produces only a further 3 per cent reduction in foetal deaths.

'Village' care (table 5). In Programme A, as a result of selective accommodation of high-risk pregnancy in the vicinity of skilled obstetric care, well-timed care is given and maternal mortality is reduced to a negligible level. The decrease in perinatal mortality will not be much greater than that of Programme A of 'standard care', but with introduction of Programme B there will be a 20 per cent reduction in deaths of newborns. As in the 'standard' obstetric care, Programme C has negligible additional effect.

Remarks

The differences in cost of prevention of death between 'standard' and 'village' care are obvious. Programme B of 'village' care is the cheapest. The increase in cost over this programme with alternative programmes is shown in table 6. While there is little difference between Programmes B and A of 'village' care the cost of prevention

Table 4
Estimated reduction in
perinatal and maternal
mortality with 'standard'
care

Reduction and cost	Programme A Antenatal care and delivery	Programme B Programme A + Transitional neonatal care for high-risk newborns	Programme C Programme A + Programme B + Intensive neonatal care
Reduction in mortality			
Perinatal reduction			
Percentage	32.3	46.9	50.0
Number	12,403	18,010	19,200
Maternal reduction			
Percentage	75.0	75.0	75.0
Number	6,000	6,000	6,000
Total reduction			
Percentage	39.7	51.7	54.3
Number	18,403	24,010	25,200
Cost (US$)			
Cost of programme	4,800,000	5,000,000	9,210,000
Cost per death prevented	261	208	366

of death increases sharply with Programme C. The cheapest programme in 'standard'
care is nearly 1.5 times that of the most expensive programme in 'village' care.

In this study, only the short-term effects of quantity and quality of perinatal
care are outlined. The long-term effects of such an undertaking cannot be
overemphasized. Additional substantial gains could continue to be made for each
successive year during which such programmes were operated.

Table 5
Estimated reduction in
perinatal and maternal
mortality with 'village'
care

Reduction and cost	Programme A Antenatal care and delivery	Programme B Programme A + Transitional neonatal care for high-risk newborns	Programme C Programme A + Programme B + Intensive neonatal care
Reduction in mortality			
Perinatal reduction			
Percentage	36.5	56.4	59.4
Number	14,076	21,658	22,810
Maternal reduction			
Percentage	95.0	95.0	95.0
Number	7,600	7,600	7,600
Total reduction			
Percentage	46.6	62.9	65.5
Number	21,616	29,258	30,410
Cost (US$)			
Cost of programme	1,100,000	1,300,000	4,408,000
Cost per death prevented	51	45	145

Table 6
Ratio of cost per death
prevented of the six
programmes described

'Standard' care	Ratio of cost	'Village' care	Ratio of cost
Programme A	5.9	Programme A	1.2
Programme B	4.7	Programme B	1.0
Programme C	8.3	Programme C	3.3

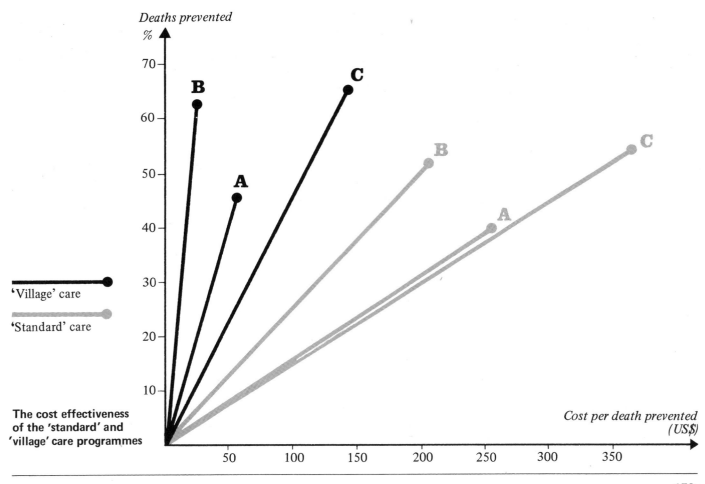

Deaths prevented
%

The cost effectiveness of the 'standard' and 'village' care programmes

'Village' care

'Standard' care

Cost per death prevented
(US$)

Nutrition

Prepared in
collaboration with
Demissie Habte

Inadequate or unbalanced intake of food is probably the most common explanatory factor behind the enormous wastage of human life at an early age in most African countries. The interaction of severe infections and undernutrition is a well-known phenomenon seemingly inescapable at present for the growing child. The most vulnerable groups are infants, young children 1 to 3 years of age and pregnant and nursing mothers. Protein-energy malnutrition (PEM) of various degrees dominates the picture. Infants are particularly sensitive since growth at their age is faster than at any other period of life, and the energy supply must thus be sufficient. Protein is the most important nutrient for growth and for repair. Carbohydrate and fat supply most of the energy needed.

Various recommendations have been made as to the necessary daily intake of nutrients for normal growth and development. Protein consumption is expressed as grams (g) per kilogram (kg) body weight, and energy need as calories (the International System of Units recommends the use of joules: 1 kcal = 4.184 kJ). A child of 1 to 3 years of age needs, for example, about 1 g of reference protein per kg and day and some 100 kcal per kg and day. A child in his first year needs about three times more protein and more than twice as many calories for each kilogram of his weight than an adult. The easiest way of assessing the growth of a child is by plotting his weight against his age on a graph. Such assessment will also be a quick, easy and fairly accurate indicator of children's health. WHO/FAO recommended in 1971 the following practical classification of nutritional status in developing countries:

1. Below 60 per cent of standard weight for age: *marasmus.*
2. 60 to 80 per cent of standard weight for age: *underweight.*
3. Oedema (swelling with water) in those below 80 per cent of standard weight for age: *kwashiorkor.*

Children become underweight and marasmic because they get too little energy-rich food. They get kwashiorkor mainly because of inadequate protein intake - usually the wrong kind of food. Kwashiorkor usually develops over a few weeks and is often fatal if the child does not receive medical attention. Marasmus, on the other hand, lasts for months or years. For every severely malnourished child there may be ten to twenty times as many moderately undernourished. In any particular community the turnover of cases of kwashiorkor will be significantly higher than that of marasmus. As Bengoa (1970) points out: 'At a given time there may be, say, two cases each of kwashiorkor and nutritional marasmus, and some three to four months later there may still be two cases of each condition, but the kwashiorkor cases are probably new cases whereas the marasmus cases are not.'

Any single country may have eradication of malnutrition as a long-term goal but it must formulate intermediate objectives. The enormous magnitude of the PEM problem prohibits its primary prevention at once, but intermediate goals must be sought. From the public-health point of view it may be possible to recognize the mild and moderate forms of PEM so that they can be prevented from developing into the easily recognizable extreme forms. The following figures were arrived at by Bengoa using information from community surveys undertaken in recent years in several countries in Africa (by point prevalence is meant the number of cases observed to have the condition at a particular point at that time):

1. Point prevalence of kwashiorkor: 0 to 1.6 per cent. Point prevalence of marasmus: 0 to 6.8 per cent. Point prevalence of kwashiorkor plus marasmus: 0 to 7.6 per cent.
2. Percentage of children with marasmus: 0.5 to 4.6 per cent.
3. Prevalence of moderate cases of PEM, mostly Gomez 2nd degree of malnutrition covering those weighing 60 to 75 per cent of the standard weight for age: 4.4 to 43.1 per cent.

It is important to note that, as Bengoa explains, 'Although the two conditions might have the same point prevalence, the number of new cases of kwashiorkor in one year may be much greater than that of nutritional marasmus.'

In a recent survey (Kidane *et al.*, 1975) of a district in Addis Ababa, disregarding the variation by age, the prevalence of marasmus was found to be 2.5 per cent and that of underweight about 30 per cent. This could be compared with figures from an MCH clinic in the same district of 4.4 per cent for marasmus, 49.3 per cent for underweight and 1.7 per cent for kwashiorkor (Freij *et al.*, 1973). An analysis of 3,500 hospital admissions to the Ethio-Swedish Paediatric Clinic showed the primary diagnosis to be 8.9 per cent with marasmus, 7.5 per cent with kwashiorkor, 1.8 per cent marasmic kwashiorkor and 5.9 per cent underweight (Tafesse, 1973).

The study

It was decided to try to estimate the cost of a programme to prevent deaths due to marasmus and kwashiorkor in a population of 10 million people with 2 million under 6 years of age. To achieve the elimination of malnutrition would be an unrealistic goal for the time being. The incidence figures given in table 7 were calculated using the figures cited above and also information on mortality in the community.

Table 7
Estimated annual morbidity and mortality in marasmus and kwashiorkor (for 2 million children between 0 and 6 years)

Disorder	Incidence (%)	Total number of cases	Case fatality of untreated cases (%)	Expected number of deaths
Marasmus	4	80,000	40	32,000
Kwashiorkor	2	40,000	50	20,000
Underweight	40	800,000	2	16,000

The cost of prevention of deaths due to kwashiorkor and marasmus may be said to constitute the sum of the cost of basic health services apportioned to child health and the cost of extra calories and protein needed. We assume that the energy and protein consumed by the children in the hypothetical country is as shown in table 8 and, calculated on the basis of available information, the cost to the child-health services to be US$3 million. This latter figure was arrived at by multiplying the operational cost of health stations/centres with the numbers needed and assuming that one-third was used for child services.

Table 8
Consumption of energy and protein (per kg body weight) at the average age of 2 years

Element consumed	Normal	Underweight	Kwashiorkor	Marasmus
Energy (kcal)	85	60	50	30
Protein (gm)	1.0	0.7	0.4	0.6

The aim of eliminating marasmus and kwashiorkor is understood to mean preventing children deteriorating from the underweight level. As we cannot select just those children that will develop the more severe stages of PEM we have to supply a larger group with additional food. In each society there may well be specific contributing factors, e.g. early weaning, measles, malaria, to take into account. Exact knowledge of the children at risk would of course give a smaller number for supplementation. However, for our exercise we assumed it necessary to treat three times as many children as actually have the severe forms of PEM. The most common and cheapest cereal-legume mixture would cost 0.0075 US cents per calorie and 0.25 US cents per gram of protein. Utilizing these figures and subtracting the calories and protein actually consumed by the child with kwashiorkor and marasmus from that of the underweight (table 8) we can calculate the additional need and the annual cost of meeting food deficiencies (table 9). The cost of preventing death calculated as cost per prevented death could be looked upon as the cost-effectiveness of this activity (table 10).

Table 9
Annual cost of meeting energy (calorie) and protein deficits in children with an average age of 2 years and weight of 8 kg

		US$			US$
1.	*To prevent kwashiorkor*		3.	*Total cost of food to*	
	(a) Cost of energy needed	262,800		*prevent kwashiorkor*	
	(b) Cost of protein needed	262,800		*and marasmus*	2,277,600
	(c) Cost of energy and protein	525,600	4.	*Reduction of cost*	1,138,800
2.	*To prevent marasmus*			*(Assuming at least 50 per cent of the extra*	
	(a) Cost of energy needed	1,576,800		*calories/proteins avail-*	
	(b) Cost of protein needed	175,200		*able at home and given)*	
	(c) Cost of energy and protein	1,752,000	5.	*Overall cost of food*	1,138,800

Calculated as follows:

1(a) *10 (60 - 50 kcal - see table 8)*
     x 8 (weight of child in kg)
x 40,000 (total number of cases - see table 7)
     x 3 (to arrive at the number of children to whom the additional calories must be given in order to reach the 40,000 who actually have the condition)
   x 365 (number of days per year)
x 0.0075 (cents per calorie)

1(b) *0.3 (0.7 - 0.4 grams - see table 8)*
     x 8 x 40,000 x 3 x 365 x 0.25 (cents)

2(a) *30 (60 - 30 kcal - see table 8)*
     x 80,000 (total number of cases - see table 7) x 8 x 3 x 365 x 0.0075 (cents)

2(b) *0.1 (0.7 - 0.6 grams - see table 8)*
     x 80,000 x 8 x 3 x 365 x 0.25 (cents)

Table 10
Cost-effectiveness of prevention of death from kwashiorkor and marasmus

Cost of preventing death from kwashiorkor and marasmus		*Number of deaths prevented*	52,000
	US$	*Cost per death prevented from kwashiorkor and marasmus*	US$80
Child-health services*	3,000,000		
Cost of food supplied	1,138,800		
	4,138,800		

Basic health services (excluding capital costs) for a population of 10 million with 2 million under 6 years of age, as an estimated portion of expenditure on basic health services totalling US$10 million (representing 200 health centres at a cost of US$30,000 per centre plus 800 health stations at a cost of US$5,000 per centre).

Remarks

We see from table 10 that in order to reduce the incidence of kwashiorkor and marasmus it is necessary to spend a total of US$ 4,138,800 each year on extra calories and protein. It has been assumed that the expected number of deaths from the two diseases would otherwise be 52,000 per year. It can, therefore, be said that the cost per death prevented is US$80. It should be emphasized that it is still possible to die from underweight even though kwashiorkor and marasmus have been prevented. It should also be noted that there are additional costs to those which have been assumed, for example the administrative costs of effecting the required distribution of food.

Immunization

Prepared in
collaboration with
Pietros Hadgu

It is possible to prevent a number of communicable diseases by active immunization, a highly specific measure for raising host resistance through the immune mechanism of the recipient. Several types of vaccines are in current use:
1. Vaccines prepared from killed causative agents (mostly bacterial and a few viral or rickettsial).
2. Vaccines prepared from attenuated or changed causative agents (a few bacterial, some rickettsial and many viral).
3. Vaccines prepared from modified bacterial products (toxin-toxoid). This type of vaccine is used only for those diseases where the toxins produced by the bacteria cause the symptom of the disease, e.g. diphtheria, tetanus.

Active immunization using live vaccines or toxoids gives a better protection of much longer duration than that of killed vaccines,which is of lower value and has a short duration. One live vaccine should not, however, be combined with another live vaccine. It is advisable to have an interval of at least three weeks between administration of live vaccines. Booster doses of live vaccines and toxoids mobilize antibodies in a very short time and in very high quantity. If, after immunization with killed vaccines, more than six months has passed, the complete vaccination should be repeated. On the other hand, the production, storage (often the vaccine should be kept at or about 4°C) and administration of live vaccines is much more complicated than that of killed vaccines. The production of toxoid vaccines is difficult, but storage and administration is easy.

For our purposes, the following vaccines will be considered:
1. *Smallpox* (a live viral vaccine). Good protection for at least three years.
2. *BCG* (live attenuated). Safe and at least 80 per cent effective in raising resistance against tuberculosis (TB). Given once, at the earliest possible age.

3. *Diphtheria/pertussis/tetanus (DPT)* (produced as a combined vaccine) is given with an interval of four weeks:
   (a) Diphtheria toxoid treated with modern absorbents provides a solid immunity.
   (b) Pertussis (whooping cough) vaccine is produced from killed bacteria.
   (c) Tetanus toxoid as for diphtheria. For protection against neonatal tetanus the pregnant mother must be immunized in the latter half of pregnancy.
4. *Poliomyelitis vaccines* are available in two forms both to be given at least three times:
   (a) Inactivated virus to be administered subcutaneously.
   (b) Live virus to be given orally. The oral vaccines usually give good protection but in some tropical countries the rate of sero-conversion may be low (John & Jayabal, 1972).
5. *Measles* vaccines also exist in two forms:
   (a) Killed virus, production of which is difficult.
   (b) Live virus, easier and less expensive to produce. The vaccination offers good protection if given after twelve months of age. Measles vaccine is still expensive, it requires refrigeration during storage and transportation, and has to be handled with great care during administration as it will be inactivated at room temperature. The epidemiologic consequences of mass vaccination can at present not be fully appreciated.

Immunization programmes as a means of disease control have been analysed as to yield of health and economic benefits from the investment of given funds (Cvjetanovic, 1973; Grundy & Reinke, 1973; Lindholm, 1973). Various mathematical and epidemiological models have been proposed, however, most often only dealing with one disease at a time.

The study

It was decided to discuss the cost of death prevention of a campaign or a series of periodic campaigns in the hypothetical country against the following five diseases:

smallpox, tuberculosis, whooping cough, polio and measles. The total population is about 10 million, of whom about 2 million are young children (0-6 years). There will be about 500,000 newborns each year and this number is used for the calculation in table 11.

Table 11 Cost per death prevented in child-death and immunization campaigns against five diseases in a population with 500,000 annual newborns

Type of vaccine	Probability of contracting the disease	Case fatality	Expected number of deaths	Number of immunizing contacts per child	Fixed cost of campaign (million US$)	Variable cost of campaign (million US$)	Total cost of campaign (million US$)	Total cost per death prevented (US$)
	(1)	(2)	(3)	(4)	(5)	(6)	(7)	(8)
Smallpox	0.005	0.1	250	1	1.0	0.025	1.025	4,100
DPT	0.1	0.05	2,500	2	2.0	0.25	2.25	900
TB	0.015	0.04	300	1	1.0	0.025	1.025	3,415
Polio	1.0	0.0005	250	3	3.0	0.375	3.375	13,500
Measles	1.0	0.16	80,000	1	1.0	0.25	1.25	16

The lack of adequate vital statistics made it necessary to come to some arbitrary compromise in order to arrive at definite numerical values which could be used for the exercise. The assumptions behind the figures in table 11, columns 1 and 2, are based on interpretation of available statistics in Ethiopia and on the experience gained in different parts of the country by senior physicians of the Ethio-Swedish Paediatric Clinic, together with data on morbidity and mortality from the now industrialized countries at a comparable stage in the past.

*Number of deaths
prevented (thousands)*

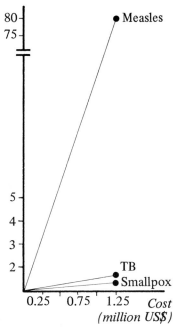

**Comparison
of the costs of measles, TB
and smallpox when all costs
are assumed to be variable**

Table 11, in which the cost per death prevented is calculated for each vaccine programme, can be seen as a cost-effective analysis, although it is highly simplified and does not claim to meet all requirements on validity and adequacy. Column 3 is the product of columns 1 and 2, assuming the target being the 500,000 newborns. Column 4 indicates the number of immunizing contacts required for the minimum protection against disease. The campaign cost is derived from the smallpox eradication programme carried out in Ethiopia during 1973. The total cost can be divided into fixed costs and variable costs, columns 5 and 6. It is assumed that once the decision has been taken to carry out a campaign then there are fixed costs for setting up the programme. These consist of, for example, cost of personnel and cost of basic equipment.

Fixed costs have been set at US$1 million for a programme which involves 1 visit per child, US$2 million for a programme which involves 2 visits per child and US$ 3 million when 3 visits per child are required. It could actually be the case that these costs are reduced proportionally as the number of visits per child is increased. Depending on the nature of the programme it is possible to regard all costs as variable. In this case cost is a linear function of the number of contacts made during a programme. The accompanying figure shows how it is possible to compare the costs of measles, TB and smallpox. The variable costs in this example, however, have been assumed to comprise vaccine and storage costs only and have been set at US$ 250,000, $25,000, and $25,000 for each vaccine, taking into consideration the number of immunizing contacts.

A critical problem in measuring the economic effects of immunization programmes is the time period being analysed. For the sake of simplicity, time is not taken into consideration here. Other assumptions are that all expected deaths can be prevented by immunization and that the only aim of a programme is to prevent as many deaths as possible.

The benefits of death prevention in terms of value of life, possible increase in production, etc. are handled as intangibles here but should, of course, implicitly be weighed against the costs for preventing death. It is not likely that a decision-maker is forced to choose between *all* or *nothing*. Therefore, it is important to think in

Table 12 Calculating the marginal cost per death prevented for measles vaccination

Number of immunizing contacts	Total fixed cost (million US$)	Total variable cost (US$)	Total cost (US$)	Number of deaths prevented	Average cost per death prevented (US$)	Increase in total cost (US$)	Increase in number of deaths prevented	Marginal cost per death prevented (US$)
1	1.0	0.5	1,000,000.50	0.16	6,250,003	-	-	3.125
5	1.0	2.5	1,000,002.50	0.8	1,250,003	2.0	0.64	3.125
10	1.0	5	1,000,005	1.6	625,003	2.5	0.8	3.125
50	1.0	25	1,000,025	8.0	125,003	20	6.4	3.125
100	1.0	50	1,000,050	16	62,503	25	8	3.125
500	1.0	250	1,000,250	80	12,503	200	64	3.125
1,000	1.0	500	1,000,500	160	6,253	250	80	3.125
2,000	1.0	1,000	1,001,000	320	3,128	500	160	3.125
5,000	1.0	2,500	1,002,500	800	1,253	1,500	480	3.125
10,000	1.0	5,000	1,005,000	1,600	628	2,500	800	3.125
20,000	1.0	10,000	1,010,000	3,200	315	5,000	1,600	3.125
50,000	1.0	25,000	1,025,000	8,000	128	15,000	4,800	3.125
100,000	1.0	50,000	1,050,000	16,000	66	25,000	8,000	3.125
200,000	1.0	100,000	1,100,000	32,000	34	50,000	16,000	3.125
300,000	1.0	150,000	1,150,000	48,000	23	50,000	16,000	3.125
400,000	1.0	200,000	1,200,000	64,000	18	50,000	16,000	3.125
500,000	1.0	250,000	1,250,000	80,000	15	50,000	16,000	3.125

terms of marginal costs. Table 12 shows how to calculate the marginal costs for the measles programme.

One of the starting points in the planning of a immunization campaign is the establishment of a schedule. The seminar working group on immunization (see the Group Observations on the Package, below) proposed the following schedule for the programme: *at 6 weeks:* TB/polio (1)/DPT (1); *at 3 to 4 months:* smallpox/polio (2)/ DPT (2); *at 1 year:* measles/polio (3). It was agreed that this was the optimal schedule of vaccinations which would satisfy the required medical conditions. It would, however, be possible to carry out a part of the schedule by making only 1 or 2 contacts instead of 3 per child. The decision about which combination of vaccines to choose depends on medical judgement and on the financial resources available. Since fixed costs have been assumed to be a high proportion of total costs and to be proportional to the number of immunizing contacts per child, the major financial decision is how many contacts to make per child.

There are a large number of alternative combinations of vaccines which can be considered, giving differing total costs of campaign. In table 13 those alternatives which give the lowest cost per death prevented are listed for each combination of number of contacts per child and number of vaccines given. If financial resources are of the order of US$1.25 million then it is clear that measles immunization gives the lowest cost per death prevented. If it is possible to finance 2 contacts per child then TB immunization could be added to the campaign. For resources between US$3 million and US$4 million, 3 contacts could be made per child and the alternative which gives the lowest cost per death prevented is TB vaccine at 6 weeks followed by smallpox at 3 to 4 months and measles at 1 year. It is worth noting, however, that DPT vaccine could be added for an additional cost of only US$0.25 million and that, similarly, polio vaccine could be added for a further US$0.375. This assumes, of course, that fixed costs vary only with the number of contacts per child and not with the number of vaccines given.

Table 13 Cost per death prevented with different combinations of vaccines

Number of immunizing contacts per child	Number of vaccines	Type of vaccine	Expected number of deaths	Fixed costs (million US$)	Variable costs (million US$)	Total costs (million US$)	Total cost per death prevented (US$)
1	1	Measles	80,000	1.0	0.250	1.250	16
2	1	DPT (1) DPT (2)	2,500	2.0	0.250	2.250	900
2	2	TB Measles	80,300	2.0	0.275	2.275	28
3	1	Polio (1) Polio (2) Polio (3)	250	3.0	0.375	3.375	13,500
3	2	DPT (1) DPT (2) Measles	82,500	3.0	0.500	3.500	42
3	3	TB Smallpox Measles	80,550	3.0	0.300	3.300	41
3	4	TB/DPT (1) Smallpox/DPT (2) Measles	83,050	3.0	0.550	3.550	43
3	5	TB/DPT (1)/polio (1) Smallpox/DPT (2)/polio (2) Measles/polio (3)	83,300	3.0	0.925	3.925	47

Remarks

It must be emphasized that this example is based on assumptions which may be questionable and that the figures arrived at are hypothetical. The costs have only been very roughly estimated for a vaccine campaign during one year. The calculation of the cost will actually depend on the period over which it is intended to maintain the campaign. Furthermore the calculations of the expected number of deaths prevented are not based on truly reliable data. In practice estimates of these figures may be very difficult to obtain. It has also been assumed that an immunization programme is 100 per cent effective and that all deaths from each disease are prevented by immunization.

In reality, the character of the country being considered is of prime importance, together with its present structure of health services. This will effect the organization of the programme and the schedule drawn up. The maintenance phase is actually the most critical, not only from an economic point of view but also from an epidemiologic one. The objective of the campaign may be one of three possibilities, eradication, control of epidemics or individual protection, and this has to be clearly stated. The decision whether or not to begin a campaign may be the most important, demanding qualified and integrated judgements from experts of several different professions.

Group Observations on the Package

The seminar participants were divided into five groups, each to discuss one item in the optimum package programme. It was intended that the groups, in so far as possible, should use the three cost-effectiveness studies presented earlier as a pattern for their exercises and that they should pay special attention to the budgeting procedure and the weighting of components within each item as well as within the package as a whole. More specifically, they were asked to centre their discussions around the following main headings: (1) objectives; (2) components: (A) identification of components involved in dealing with each item of the optimum package programme; (B) internal priority rating of measures proposed; (C) cost of each component; (3) priority rating of each item within the whole optimum package programme; (4) methods of implementation of proposed measures: (a) planning; (b) organization; (c) manpower and development. The reports of the groups are printed below in somewhat abbreviated form, with some editorial comment. It is felt that in spite of the sketchiness, reflecting the lack of time available to the groups at the seminar, the reports do provide a valuable consensus and also a model for collaborative discussion of the package plan.

Social Inputs

Group 1
E.A. Yoloye (chairman)
J.J. Kisa (rapporteur)
B.B.A. Asirifi
P. Asiyo
Assefa Mehretu
E.F.P. Jelliffe
B. Lukutati
T.P. Omari
Teshome Wagaw

Taking the three areas of preparation of parents for parenthood, family welfare and child-spacing, and the socialization process together, Group 1 defined objectives in these three areas as follows:
1. To create awareness among parents regarding their roles and responsibilities in effective parenthood in order to ensure the sound physical, psychological and social development of their children.
2. To create conditions which are conducive to the effective functioning of the family through the efforts of its members as well as those of external agencies.
3. To ensure the transmission to the child of that culture which is appropriate for effective living in the society in which the child is born or in which the child will eventually live.

Components A

1. *Preparation of parents.* Responsible parenthood would require a package of measures which could be classed as 'education'. They would include: (a) food and nutrition education; (b) child care and development (child feeding, hygiene and sanitation, clothing, preventive care and use of available maternal and child-health services, which would include family planning where called for); (c) family relations within the nuclear family as well as the extended family; (d) child development from conception to age 6; (e) family economics.
2. *Family welfare.* The improvement of family welfare would depend on the provision of the following services: (a) education; (b) health; (c) community development and social welfare; (d) agricultural extension; (e) transport.
3. *Socialization.* The proper socialization of the child would require a two-pronged education approach aimed respectively at parents and at children. The programme for the parents would include good citizenship, literacy and leadership as its main ingredients while the pre-school children's programme would centre around social interaction, cultural activities and social and cultural services.

B   1. *Preparation of parents.* The order of priority of the proposed measures for preparation of parents was as follows: (a) food and nutrition education; (b) child care; (c) family relations; (d) child development; (e) family economics.
2. *Family welfare.* The proposed measures concerning family welfare were placed in the following order: (a) health services; (b) education; (c) agricultural extension; (d) transport; (e) community development and social welfare.
3. *Socialization.* Concerning this part of the item the order agreed upon was (a) education, (b) social and cultural activities.
It should be noted that of all the measures proposed, education in its broadest sense was assigned first priority, health second priority, social welfare and community development third priority, and transport fourth.

C   From the data on the hypothetical country, Group 1 concluded that the total number of children and mothers needing attention under the programme was 3,600,000. The per capita expenditure of the ministry of health was given at US$2. Allocating 50 per cent of this on a *per capita* basis to Group 1's item, the figure of US$3,600,000 was arrived at, which represents 18 per cent of the total health budget. These funds were allocated to the four broad items in accordance with their priorities as follows: (a) education, 40 per cent (US$1,440,000); (b) health, 30 per cent (US$1,080,000); (c) social welfare and community development, 20 per cent (US$720,000); (d) transport, 10 per cent (US$360,000); total, US$3,600,000.

Priorities within the package

Group 1 rated the social inputs as first priority within the whole optimum package programme because it was considered that if the measures proposed were implemented and the objectives achieved, Groups 2, 3, 4 and 5 would have the gravity of their problems considerably reduced.

Methods of implementation

Implementation was proposed in the following way:
Planning. (a) Taking stock of the problems facing parents and their children.

Public health education - not just for mothers!

(b) Taking an inventory of existing facilities and services. (c) Evaluating available manpower and its deployment. (d) Setting targets. (e) Formulating measures and projects. (f) Allocating funds to the measures and projects for both capital and recurrent expenditure in accordance with their respective priorities.

Organization. The strategy would be to (a) integrate all services provided to ensure complementary effectiveness; (b) place emphasis on rural areas; (c) plan adequate transport for the sparsely populated areas, perhaps by mobile units; (d) make use of existing facilities, such as schools; (e) involve local opinion leaders in the campaign; (f) experiment with a model demonstration package (see diagram).

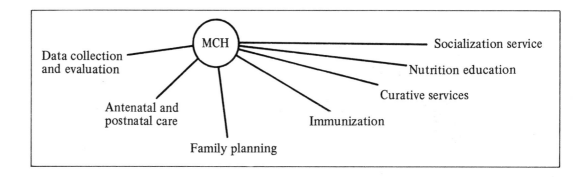

Comment   The group emphasized the importance of education in its broadest sense and ranked it as number 1 in the internal priority list. There has, however, been some discussion about how new education works as an innovation vehicle for health. Read (1966), for example, has pointed out that universal education is no sure road to a scientific acceptance of preventive health practices ('. . . most of the evidence seems to show that school education is slow to affect people's belief about their bodies and their health') and that it is probably a mistake to expect a scientific outlook from the majority of people in any country since the distinction in all countries is between the specialists in health and the rest of the people. The general population looks upon health as being equivalent to the absence of disease that prohibits work (Long, 1972). Do, in fact, knowledge and attitudes have to be changed before a change in behaviour can be observed? It has generally been emphasized that education should be culturally acceptable. Yet, according to Molnos (1972), 'there should not be an over-emphasis on traditional cultural material, since it is important to consider the dynamic nature of society and the accompanying structural changes in beliefs and practices'.

Perinatal Care

Group 2

B. Vahlquist (chairman)
O. Ransome-Kuti
(rapporteur)
R. Iliasu
V.P. Kimati
M. Mufwaya
Nebiat Tafari
E. Odotei
M.L. Oduori
A. Catipovic

A review of the problems in various countries was given by members of the team. Broadly, the problems were as follows:

Antenatal care. In most African countries the antenatal services available to the majority of women were either in health centres/hospitals in the big towns or in rural health centres. The service was mainly by midwives or a less trained medical auxiliary.

Labour. Thirty to 60 per cent of women delivered their babies in an institution. Perinatal mortality rates ranged from 37/1000 in one maternity hospital in Nigeria to 63/1000 in a community in Ghana and 112/1000 in an Ethiopian hospital. Common problems encountered were: (a) in the antenatal period: disproportion, eclampsia, nutritional deficiencies, anaemia, antepartum haemorrhage, ectopic gestation; (b) during labour: malposition, uterine inertia, etc.; (c) newborns: prematurity, asphyxia neonatorum, neonatal tetanus, neonatal jaundice, infections (conjunctivitis, hypoglycaemia, hypothermia, etc.).

The objectives were defined as:
1. To provide antenatal care for all pregnant women in the community, i.e. 500,000/ year.
2. Facilities for all pregnant women to be attended during labour by medical personnel.
3. Facilities for high-risk mothers to be accommodated in a maternity village before labour with delivery of these mothers in hospitals, with an observation unit for high-risk infants.

Components

A It was felt that facilities for at least three visits for each pregnant woman at the health centre should be provided for. The high-risk group should also be given a

The importance of prenatal care

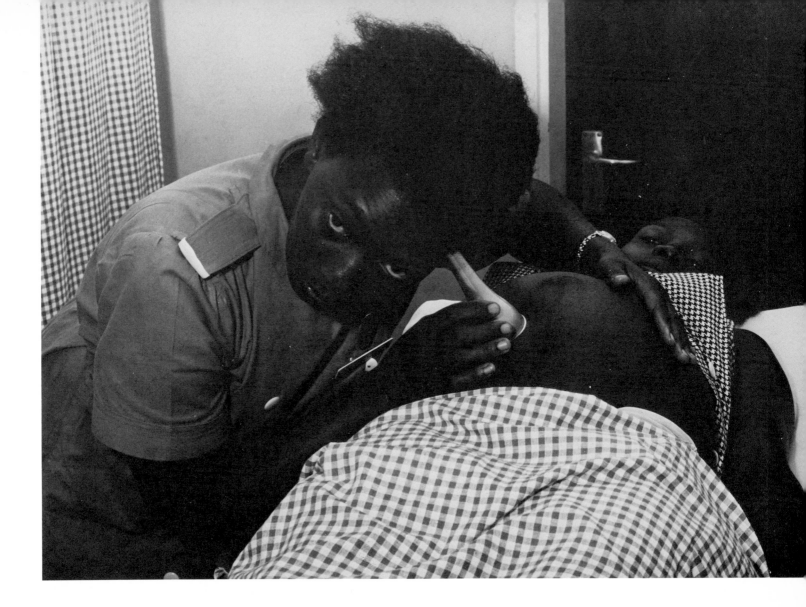

more detailed examination. At one of the visits, a decision would be taken whether or not they should be transferred to the district hospital for specialized attention. At the hospital, they would be housed in a maternity village until delivery. Throughout pregnancy mothers would be given antimalarials, vitamins and iron, immunization with tetanus toxoid, supplementary food, and health education, particularly on the importance of breast-feeding.

Mothers designated as at no risk would normally be delivered at home but under certain circumstances the health centre could also be used. Whoever attends to deliver the baby must be adequately trained to deal with neonatal emergencies (particularly asphyxia neonatorum), care of the umbilical cord, and prevention of hypothermia and neonatal infections. It is recommended that each rural health centre should be staffed by two midwives and six health auxiliaries to provide a 24-hour service. Only 30 per cent of the time of the staff would be used in delivering these services. One rural health centre should be constructed for 50,000 people.

B   For at-risk mothers it is estimated that 25 per cent of hospital beds should be provided. Of the high-risk pregnancies (10 per cent of the total included) only a few will produce babies in need of intensive care, and ideally there should be a number of small units for intensive care of babies spread over the country.

C   Antenatal care and delivery costs would be broken down as follows:

Antenatal care (a)   Antenatal care for 500,000 pregnancies: three visits x 500,000 = 1,500,000 antenatal visits
Cost of visits (at $0.40) = $600,000

(b)   High-risk pregnancy for 50,000 (10 per cent of 500,000): maternity village stay of 15 days at $0.50/woman/day = $375,000

Care during labour Delivery and five days in hospital for 50,000 high-risk mothers at $3/day (average for all pregnancies) = $750,000
(Since the cost of hospital stay will be included in another item of expenditure in the ministry, this item should be substituted in the total.)
Delivery at home or at health centre at $2 for 450,000 pregnancies = $900,000

Therefore, the total for perinatal care = $1,875,000

Priorities within the package

Priorities were determined on the basis of deciding which of the programmes would have the most effect in reducing the infant mortality rate. In this respect, it seems clear that since the largest number of deaths, as shown by Ethiopian figures, occurs in the perinatal period, the order of priorities should be as follows:
1. Perinatal care.
2. Nutrition in infancy and childhood.
3. Immunization and other preventive measures.
4. Hygiene and environmental sanitation.
5. Social inputs.

Comment

As is evident from the perinatal care study above and the group report a programme of improved perinatal care would be one of the most powerful tools in dramatically reducing infant mortality rates in countries with very high levels. Such a programme will work only on the at-risk concept: 'our aim should be services which are comprehensive in scope but "at risk" in focus' (Jelliffe & Jelliffe, 1972). The degree of community involvement in such a programme would be considerable and it should be emphasized that the chain leading to rural health care must begin and not end in the community. Village involvement should usually start very early, during the planning stage, and an active involvement by the community should be encouraged.

For the villager, the prevention of death has probably the most significant effect and this should therefore remain the primary aim of health services.

Most health problems of infants and young children have to be approached through the mother, and the importance of her role cannot be overemphasized. In the study of 1,000 families in the UK (Spence et al, 1954) it was observed that in attempting to correlate the health of the children to their environment one dominating factor emerged: the capacity of the mother. Maternal ill-health has profound influence on the physical, emotional and social health of the children as well as on the work output of the immediate family.

The amount of curative treatment and diagnostic endeavour in a package programme needs careful thinking and will obviously have to vary from place to place. The existing tools are quite effective; if contemporary drugs could be made available, an intelligent villager, trained to recognize the two or three most prevalent local ailments, may be able to do more to save lives and end sickness than the best doctor could have done twenty-five years ago. Treatment may be simple and basic, but also effective and cheap, and it may provide an important incentive for people also to take up the preventive aspect of the package.

Nutrition

Group 3
D.B. Jelliffe (Chairman)
Mehari Gebre-Medhin
(Rapporteur)
Demissie Habte
M. Fischer
G. Lundgren
D.J. Njau
S.K. Ongeri
Solomon Ayalew
I. Thomas

The nutrition programme outlined below pivots on the health station, which should be looked upon as a multipurpose service centre. All the activities of the centre, of which nutrition is only one, would under normal circumstances be planned in integration.

The main target group of the programme was taken to be infants and children between the ages of 6 months and 3 years. Infants below 6 months were given second priority, on the assumption that the nutritional needs of this age group would be adequately met by breast-feeding. In infants and in children PEM, iron-deficiency anaemia and vitamin A deficiency were taken as the main nutritional problems. The following prevalence figures were used as a basis for planning: mild-moderate PEM 40 per cent, kwashiorkor 2 per cent, marasmus 2 per cent, iron-deficiency anaemia 10 per cent, vitamin A deficiency 0.5 per cent.

Assuming that 10 per cent of the population would be below 3 years the number of infants and children under consideration for the programme would be approximately 1 million. It is assumed that this figure remains constant throughout the programme implementation period of five years. The general objectives of the programme may be described as the provision of optimum package services with paramedical personnel in a rural setting in order to eradicate all forms of severe PEM and vitamin A deficiency and to reduce iron-deficiency anaemia to a minimum. The programme would also include provision for the management of early cases, so that a considerable decrease in the prevalence of mild-moderate PEM could be achieved. In more precise terms eradication of kwashiorkor and marasmus would be achieved by aiming at a yearly decrease in these syndromes of 0.5 per cent for a period of five years. Iron-deficiency anaemia would be brought down to the asymptotic value of 2 per cent per annum.

Components

A The most important ingredients in the nutrition element of the optimum package programme were felt to be as follows: (a) health education: breast-feeding (and the dangers of bottle-feeding), weaning practices, dietary advice; and (b) child-care management: identification of at-risk factors, weight measurement, height measurement.

B Health education, serial weighing and supplementary food on strict indications are looked upon as indispensable items which should be given foremost priority.

C The following cost items were identified:

	US$		US$
1. Weight charts for 1,000,000 infants and children (at 4.5 cents per chart)	45,000	7. Manpower: 1,000 community health aides (87,500 x 12)	1,050,000
2. 1,000 weighing machines for infants and children (at $35 per machine)	35,000	2,000 village-level workers (50,000 x 12)	600,000
3. 1,000 weighing machines for mothers (at $7.5 per machine)	7,500	Cooking and demonstration facilities, light, water (7,500 x 12)	90,000
4. Supplementary food (see below)	91,000	8. Transport (ten visits per year to 1,000 health stations at	
5. Vitamin A	2,000	$12 per visit)	144,000
6. Iron	2,000	Total	2,066,500

Supplementary food. During the first year a total of 13,000 kwashiorkor-affected and marasmic children would receive supplements for twenty days each. The cost is determined by assuming a 10 kg child consuming 3 g/kg protein per day obtained from a currently available, commercially produced supplementary food (cost: approximately 25 cents).

**Nutrition:
Not just quantity but
also what to eat**

Priorities within the package

It was proposed that this programme be given 40 per cent of the total resources for the package, thus being considered the most urgent by the group.

Methods of implementation

Planning. Costing of programme, definition of staff requirement, definition of health-station requirement per population.
Organization. Supervision by health-centre staff, development of referral system from health station to health centre.
Manpower development. Recruitment of the new cadres of health workers (see Component C), organization of training courses, restraint in recruitment of costly professionals, including doctors.

Comment

Reluctance to appreciate that malnutrition, often equivalent to starvation, exists in the age group 6 months to 3 years is understandable in psychological and political terms, since malnourished children in rural villages or urban slums are not usually seen by administrators and policy-makers. Unicef (1973) concluded that there was a need in the less-developed countries to establish permanent supplementary feeding programmes for the young child. The basis for this recommendation is not to be found in documented experience, which is still very limited. With the present detrimental general tendency to earlier and earlier weaning of infants, supplementary feeding programmes may well have adverse effects. Such side-effects of innovations have to be taken into account. It is believed (Mönckeberg, 1973) that, 'as a rule, the extension of health services to the less privileged groups has had a detrimental effect on the incidence and duration of breast-feeding. When socio-economic conditions are unsatisfactory, distribution of milk, even free distribution, does not prevent malnutrition'.

The Zagreb guidelines state that nutrition education should be a priority in all health services. There is, however, surprisingly little evidence either that existing techniques of nutritional education are as effective as is generally assumed or that they represent a good utilization of limited resources; it appears that many conventional programmes have not succeeded in influencing food habits in a desirable direction. In evaluating the nutritional education of the community and in developing guidelines for the future, the adequacy of the teaching methods used, of the content of the programme and of the methods used for evaluation must be considered. In judging the response to a nutritional education programme, it should be borne in mind that poverty and other constraints may prevent people from responding to advice on food habits (WHO, 1972).

There is a tendency for 'nutrition', even in its many new shapes, to be still too much associated with the negative side of the picture, malnutrition, for it to make the needed breakthrough as a priority in development. Concentration upon nutritional inadequacies has also diverted attention from the real food value of some local diets and from the human need for enjoyment in eating, which has been largely ignored in nutrition planning.

Immunization

Group 4
A.O. Lucas (chairman)
S. Ofosu-Amaah
(rapporteur)
G. Arhammar
O. Gish
G. Hedenström
Y.K. Libakeni
Mesfin Demissie
Pietros Hadgu
A.H. Thomas
K. Zahir

Within the general hypothetical-country framework, it was assumed, for the sake of calculation, that 15 per cent of the population were living in urban areas, 45 per cent living in rural areas with rural health-care institutions within a distance of 10 km ('Rural I'), and 30 per cent of the population living in the rural areas within a distance of 10 to 20 km from any health institution ('Rural II'). The remaining 10 per cent were assumed to have no regular access to health service. It was also assumed that the urban areas were covered by hospitals and urban health centres, while the rural sector had health centres and/or health posts or dispensaries. The health centre had a staff of ten health workers, and the health post or dispensary a staff of two health workers.

The functions of a rural health centre would comprise curative work, midwifery, child care, immunization, nutrition, health education, family planning, environmental health, record-keeping and referral, while those of a health post or dispensary would be MCH, including immunization, curative work, sanitation, record-keeping and referral. The main causes of death for consideration in the immunization programme are premature delivery, pertussis, measles, malaria, neonatal tetanus, tuberculosis, poliomyelitis and smallpox.

The general objective of the immunization programme would be to reduce the mortality rate from 150 to 50 per 1000 for infants and from 20 to 5 per 1000 for the age group 1 to 4 years. The specific objective for immunization and other preventive measures would be to reach 70 to 80 per cent of children born. It is expected that the targets of the programme would be achieved within five years.

Failure to immunize may ruin a life

Immunization procedures would be adopted to reduce morbidity and mortality from tuberculosis, smallpox, measles, DPT and polio; and in addition, malarial prophylaxis to pregnant women to reduce that portion of prematurity attributable to malaria, together with the reduction of deaths due to malaria and diarrhoea in children. The enabling or intermediate objective would be to ensure that the health institutions already described exist (and function normally) and that through health education and community mobilization people would use these institutions. It was expected that over 80 per cent of the children would be reached in the urban areas, while 70 to 80 per cent may be conveniently reached in Rural I, and 60 to 70 per cent of the children with 'outreach' or mobile clinic in Rural II. In other areas special campaigns may have to be mounted to reach some of these areas. In summary this means that 70 per cent of children would be reached.

Components

A

Vaccines	Cost per child (cents)	Vaccines	Cost per child (cents)
1. BCG	5	7. Tetanus toxoid (twice) to mother	5
2. Smallpox			90
3. Polio (four times)	40	8. Pyrimethamine to mother	
4. DPT (three times)	15		10
5. Measles	20	Total	100 cents
6. DT (once)	5		

Malaria death prevention (in chloroquine to the child) would cost an additional 15 cents per child.

Immunization regimen. The rationale here is to reduce the visits to the health institution to the minimum and to combine the programme as much as possible with other things from which the mother and child may benefit while attending, at the same time ensuring the scientific efficacy of the programme. The alternative regimens are:

I. *Child*
		Mother
Birth	BCG Smallpox	Last half of pregnancy:
2 months	Polio DPT (1)	Tetanus toxoid (twice)
3 months	Polio DPT (2)	Weekly during the last twelve weeks:
4 months	Polio DPT (3)	Pyrimethamine
9 months		
to 1 year	Measles	
3 to 5 years	DT booster	
	Polio booster	

This regimen, with six visits at least, allows for constant supervision of development, but is expensive in mother time and has a tendency to reduce the actual number of visits.

II.
6 weeks (postnatal visit):	BCG/Polio/DPT
3 to 4 months:	Smallpox/Polio/DPT
1 year:	Measles/Polio/DPT
3 to 5 years:	DT/Polio booster

Regimen II was found attractive for these reasons: (a) BCG and smallpox can be used as markers for the first two visits; (b) the number of visits is reduced to only three in the first year; (c) the postnatal visit at 6 weeks would be the opportunity to help the mother with family-planning needs, e.g. discussing and fitting the loop, checking on the status of the umbilical stump and ensuring that breast-feeding is well established (this visit is a critical one in the MCH programme); (d) the second visit would be the opportunity to start discussing supplementary feeding from 4 months, diarrhoea prevention and the management of fever.

B   The priority rating within the immunization programmes was seen as follows: (1) BCG; (2) smallpox (country-wide maintenance) phase; (3) DPT; (4) measles (for specific problems of maintenance phase, see page 195); (5) polio.

Priorities within the package

Priority ratings within the whole package programme were seen as (1) social inputs, (2) nutrition, (3) sanitation, (4) immunization, (5) perinatal care.

Methods of implementation

Planning. Demographic data, epidemiological data, and data on the distribution of health institutions and their catchment areas are needed, together with knowledge of where to obtain constant and cheap supplies of vaccines, drugs and other ancillary material.

Organization of programme. The organization of the programme would imply the following measures: community mobilization; strategic zonal distribution of supplies from a central depot; supply and maintenance of essential refrigerators in the health institutions; constancy of supplies by careful monitoring of distribution; utilization of vaccines; incorporation of the immunization programme in the normal routines of the centres, so that they are not separate 'campaigns'; and a system of assessment and evaluation (e.g. (a) a simple system for notifying infectious disease, (b) maintaining a list of notifiable diseases, (c) simple record-keeping of numbers immunized, and the number completing each set of immunizations, and (d) a record of possible failures in vaccines used). The need for periodic supervision by the district medical officer and his senior staff is paramount. For long-term evaluation, there is need to have some system of vital events registration.

Manpower development. The members of the health team should be trained in the uses, techniques and problems of immunization and the senior district supervisory staff should continue to give in-service training at appropriate times.

In reviewing a national immunization programme it is clear that the cost of the vaccines themselves is not the major constraint on success but rather the organization of the health infrastructure, the motivation of health workers as well as the community, the overcoming of problems of distance, and regular evaluation of the service.

It is advisable that the programme, once accepted and put into operation, should be carried out indefinitely.

Comment It would be proper in this context to stress that it is not at all clear how many children in a given community are brought to utilize health facilities for vaccination, and a definite effect on the pattern of communicable diseases does not seem to have been obtained. The continuing high rate of refusal of vaccination, even where facilities are abundant, and the high drop-out rate may have more far-reaching implications than is generally thought. Thus it has been observed in a field trial of cholera vaccine that both morbidity and mortality rates were significantly higher in the 'refusal' group than in either the control group or the vaccinated group (Azurin & Alvero, 1971). This would indicate that the 'refusal' group is basically different from the control group. Reasons for refusal of vaccination should thus be taken into account when immunization programmes are planned.

The detrimental effect on the health-care system of mounting disease-specific national campaigns is now clear, from the point of view of both the failure of eradication campaigns and the cost-effective criteria (see the cost-effectiveness study on immunization, page 166). Large schemes of this kind divert money from the important horizontal integrated maintenance phase in controlling the disease. As regards measles vaccination there are further problems of vaccine storage and handling as well as the necessity continuously to reach at least 95 per cent of a community to control outbreaks of epidemics. The price of measles vaccination is also still prohibitively high and this should be an area for inputs by the technology of the industrialized countries. In spite of the high death toll of measles, a decision to immunize against the disease on a large scale must be based on a fully informed assessment of the relevant factors. (For further references, see Woodruff, 1975.)

Environmental Sanitation

Group 5
Maaza Bekele (chairman)
F.P. Okediji
E.M. Bakoja
A.D. Chiduo
A.K. Joppa
S. Kanani
Li Pao-ai
Lin Chuan-chia

It was assumed that most of the diseases (roughly about 75 per cent) which are prevalent in the hypothetical country, such as all forms of parasitic diseases, dysentery, cholera, etc., are explained by the poor environmental sanitation in this particular country. Some indicators point to the plausibility of this assumption - low *per capita* income, high infant mortality rate, location of most of the health facilities in the cities, and the poverty of the rural areas - and the discussion is based on this assumption.

The objectives of the optimum package programme are to reduce the high infant mortality rate by 75 per cent within a relatively short period of time. They were narrowed down to the provision of the following: supply of water; arrangements for refuse and excreta disposal; drainage system; food handling measures; and improvement in the general living conditions, including personal hygiene promotion.

Components　　A　The components may be further described in the following way:
Water. Special emphasis would be placed on the improvement of the quality of water supply. This would entail the protection of sources of water supply, including wells, springs and rivers, to avoid contamination. Wells should be covered, and they should not be sited close to latrines, refuse and excreta-disposal depots and graveyards. Springs and wells should be enclosed; rivers should be divided with respect to utilization (e.g. specific areas should be allotted for washing clothes and other household materials, and others for the use of cattle). Water from such sources should be boiled, and chlorination ought to be carried out to clean the water.
Refuse and excreta disposal and drainage. Latrines, incinerators and compost-pits should be provided for disposal of refuse. Decomposed or burnt remains can be used as manures.

Simple hygiene may save lives
(but the towel may spread diseases)

Food handling. Covering materials should be provided for foods sold for public consumption (as in markets and roadside stalls). Storage facilities for foods from farms or homes to markets and back to farms or homes are necessary to preserve the high quality of food made available for public consumption. Thorough inspection of foods, coupled with health and personal cleanliness on the part of those handling food, are necessary. Flies should be eliminated. Poultry, cattle, goats and sheep ought to be raised on farms rather than within compounds or on streets.
Personal hygiene and general living conditions. Houses should not be built crowded together, adequate ventilation should be provided to allow adequate use of natural sunlight, and personal cleanliness should be imperative. An organized programme of public education should support the whole gamut of the action programme.

B   The highest internal priority rating of measures proposed is the training of the sanitarians, who would function at the village level to implement (in collaboration with the villagers) the action programme.

C   It is proposed that the ratio of sanitarians to population should be 1:5,000 and 2,000 sanitarians would therefore be needed, at the rate of 400 on the ground per year. The minimum qualification for admission to be trained as a sanitarian should be six years of primary school. The training period to assume the status of a sanitarian is eighteen months, and the salary proposed is US$40 per month plus 20 per cent for operational costs (such as, for example, the provision of bicycles) plus one-third of the salary of the sanitarian for capital costs. The total cost would be US$ 510,000 a year with fixed annual increases.

Priorities within the package

Environmental sanitation and hygiene is ranked highest because of the great reduction (by 75 per cent) of infant mortality in a relatively short period foreseen by the group.

**Methods of
implementation**

Planning. The organizational structure of the village community should be activated for planning purposes. The planning body should be the village council and the necessary financial and material resources should be provided by the district council. *Organization.* The sanitarian should involve chiefs, teachers, religious heads and other types of opinion leaders in the village council. All the inhabitants of the village should be motivated so that they will be collectively involved in all aspects of the action programme. The benefits to the villages to be derived from these action programmes must be emphasized.
Manpower development. Three categories of manpower will be needed: sanitarian, supervisor and sanitary technician.

Sanitarians are the action men at the village-level who will be trained to perform multi-purpose functions. The supervisors should be technically trained. One supervisor will supervise twenty sanitarians. The supervisor should be trained to collect statistics, evaluate the data collected and feed such data to the district council for further transmission. Sanitary technicians will give technical advice and help to the sanitarians working at the village level. A training institute would be needed to train the different categories of manpower. An evaluation unit should be built into the training institute.

Comment

As is evident from the report the provision of domestic water received considerable attention in the discussion. It should perhaps not be treated as an economic good, but rather be regarded as a basic right of every member of society. The water supply should be of acceptable quality and adequate quantity at all times and at a price that can be afforded. What is acceptable quality? How much is an adequate quantity? Is there a minimum level? What are the dividends for individual and community health from improved water supply? What are the least costly means of meeting whatever is regarded as minimum health standards? We see from table 14 (Bradley, 1974) that different diseases respond to either increased quality or increased quantity of water and that in rural areas quantity may be the more important, while in peri-urban zones quality may be crucial.

Table 14
Classification of infective diseases in relation to water supplies (Bradley, 1974)

Category	Examples	Relevant water improvements
I Water-borne infections		
(a) Classical	Typhoid, cholera	Microbiological sterility
(b) Non-classical	Infective hepatitis	Microbiological improvement
II Water-washed infections		
(a) Skin and eyes	Scabies, trachoma	Greater volume available
(b) Diarrhoeal diseases	Bacillary dysentery	Greater volume available
III Water-based infections		
(a) Penetrating skin	Schistosomiasis	Protection of user
(b) Ingested	Guinea worm	Protection of source
IV Infections with water-related vectors		
(a) Biting near water	Sleeping sickness	Water piped from source
(b) Breeding in water	Yellow fever	Water piped to site of use

The Effort to Achieve a Synthesis

Weighting of Components in the Package

This section was prepared on the basis of summaries provided by Yngve Larsson and Oscar Gish.

It was felt that the problem of public health planning for African children, of finding the balance between quality, quantity and cost, was almost identical to the more general problem posed by Bryant (1973), among others, of how to use limited resources to provide effective health care for large numbers of people. The health-care system has been allowed to become so extremely inefficient that even a small amount of common sense applied to the situation will carry it very far in the direction everyone wants it to go. The interrelated character of the approaches to the solution of child-health problems has already been stressed elsewhere. The importance of planning for children lies in ensuring that the various actions affecting the condition and development of children are weighed and decided upon simultaneously and in relation to each other.

No proposal for an optimum package could be said to be final; nor, indeed, could it be much more than hypothetical until it had been tried out in practice. The results of such testing, moreover, through designed packages in the future or through retrospective analyses intended to elicit those elements in past medical programmes that are capable of useful interpretation for consideration in the structuring of present projects, are not likely to be conclusive in any absolute sense and, what is more to the point, are not likely to provide useful 'hard' material in the immediate future. Tomorrow's conclusions from today's conditions may not be valid in the dynamically evolving social setting.

None the less, it was felt that the urgency of the present situation should be matched by an equal urgency in the search for a solution. The package programme is therefore evoked - a pragmatic optimum package intended to maximize the value to be drawn from the limited resources available. If there was agreement on this and on what component elements should be included in the programme, there was less agreement on the weighting of each element therein. If there are limited resources, how much of the budget should be devoted to nutrition, say, compared with immunization? Relative weighting between more than two elements is yet more difficult to resolve. The results of the discussions of these questions and of the practical problems of delivering such programmes are pursued below.

The group decides

In the guidelines for group work, each group was asked to rate its component or topic according to priority within the optimum package programme. All but one of the five groups felt that their component of the package was the most important. The common denominator used by the four groups was the power of their programme in reducing the infant mortality rate. However, the motivation given by the group working on the social inputs (preparation of parents for parenthood, family welfare and the socialization process) was that if the measures proposed by them were implemented and the objectives achieved the gravity of the problems facing the other groups would be very much reduced. Disregarding the obvious and considerable overlap between the five components, particularly with regard to staff utilization, educational activities and community orientation, a ranking list was arrived at by empirical discussion at the seminar. The order was as follows:

1. Nutrition.
2. Social inputs.
3. Hygiene and environmental sanitation.
4. Immunization.
5. Perinatal care.

Setting priorities

A less hit-and-miss method would depend upon the more precise determination of priorities. A useful technique has been proposed by Bryant (see table 15). Four criteria are used: prevalence, or the frequency with which the problem occurs; seriousness, that is, the destructiveness of the problem for individuals and society; community concern, which includes the knowledge, attitudes and feelings of urgency about a problem; and vulnerability to management, which takes into account the availability of methods for managing the problem as well as the costs and effectiveness of applying them. In the absence of numerical data, these criteria are weighted intuitively as shown in the table.

An attempt to apply this type of approach to the problem of priorities within the optimum package programme is shown in table 16. For each of these criteria each of the five package components was given a score from 1 to 4, and the total score was developed by multiplying score values. The ranking order from this exercise was completely different from the previous one, i.e.
1. Immunization.
2. Perinatal care.
3. Hygiene and environmental sanitation.
4. Nutrition.
5. Social inputs.
One conclusion of the exercise was that activities with far-reaching goals leading to fundamental changes of social structures, however important they might be, would

have less chance of competing with programmes of a limited span. Local criteria might alter the weighting of elements in such a way as to give the radical programme more chance of realization, and it should be noted in this connexion that the priorities need to be locally approved, in any case, in order for the package to be problem-specific. But feasibility and, possibly, permanence of effect should be major

Table 15
Criteria for building priorities (after Bryant, 1969)

Health problems	Prevalence	Seriousness	Community concern	Vulnerability to management	Totals
Overly large and poorly spaced families	+ + + +	+ + + +	+ + +	+ +	96
Inadequate antenatal and obstetrical care	+ + + +	+ +	+ +	+ + +	48
Malnutrition	+ + +	+ + +	+ +	+ +	36
Needs for medical care	+ +	+ +	+ + + +	+ +	32
Communicable diseases of children	+	+ + + +	+ +	+ +	16
Specific diseases					
Malaria	+	+ + +	+ + +	+ +	18
Venereal diseases	+ +	+ +	+ +	+ +	16
Dental problems	+ + + +	+	+ +	+ +	16
Tuberculosis	+	+ + +	+ +	+ +	12
Leprosy	+	+ +	+ + +	+	6
Common cold	+	+	+	+	1
Yaws	−	+ +	+ + +	+ + + +	0

*Score developed by multiplying pluses ( ). Multiplying is necessary to remove problems with low prevalence (yaws) and low vulnerability (common cold) from priority contention.

determinants. There is no point in carrying out immunization and other measures for one population cohort only; if these are not followed up by the necessary repeats and programmes for successive generations, then the effect will not be lasting and the value of the investment will be jeopardized.

Table 16 A proposal for relative weighting of the five components of the optimum package programme, by Yngve Larsson

Criteria	Social inputs	Perinatal care	Nutrition	Immunization	Hygiene and environmental sanitation
1. Prevalence of the problem	4	4	4	3	4
2. Seriousness of the problem	4	4	4	4	4
3. Community concern for the problem	2	1	2	3	2
4. Problem's vulnerability to management	2	3	2	3	2
5. Importance of programme for survival	1	4	2	2	3
6. Importance of programme for normal growth and development	3	3	4	3	3
7. Feasibility of programme within public health resources	2	3	2	4	2
8. Coverage, efficiency of programme (input/output/time)	2	3	2	4	2
Totals (product)	768	5,184	2,048	10,368	2,304
Ranking order	5	2	4	1	3

It is important to be clear about feasibility and degree of achievement. Some disappointment over the lack of impact of past programmes may be explained by failure to recognize at the outset that only certain degrees of achievement were possible in given situations. This suggests that programmes should be rated at the outset in terms of their maximum potential. Miracle solutions are not available and a programme with a fair degree of achievement possibility, in cost-effectiveness terms, for the five package components may yet fail to reach its optimum level, because of a transport/delivery problem, for instance. This should be confronted realistically as a clear hazard before the programme starts and the recognition of its importance to implementation might be expressed in percentage terms. Thus, the potential of a particular programme might be rated within a 40 to 60 per cent range. It should then be possible to work back from this sort of evaluation in social-effectiveness terms to provide more meaningful contributions to the planning process.

Delivering the Package

The planning problem

The participants at the Addis Ababa seminar had two important observations in mind when considering the problems of delivery, first, that a moderately good plan implemented is far superior to a perfect plan gathering dust on a shelf, and second, that 80 per cent of failures in socio-economic plans are due to administrative deficiencies (Hilleboe *et al.,* 1972). Those governments that are in best control of resource allocation - in practice, this means those countries whose economies are farthest from the unrestrained free-enterprise model - are also best able to plan and best placed to execute the plan when drafted, though they may suffer from some structural rigidities.

There is an enormous literature on planning and the crisis in planning (see Seers, 1972), and new approaches to it are still being made. The wealth of literature on planning illustrates, among other things, the belief in the rational use of resources and in the need to improve on *ad hoc* decisions. Unfortunately, in practice, most national long-term plans run out of steam somewhat after the first year or two as circumstances alter and as politicians change and the annual plan becomes very often the only real plan that people can work with. As such, it is very much an *ad hoc* instrument.

In the competition for more financial resources, those who believe in integrated planning for children may benefit from the argument put forward by Savosnick (1972) for nutrition programmes, that if the ministry of health is so convinced of the benefits of improved nutrition that they are willing to cut down on other health programmes, they will really convince the Treasury of the importance of the subject and of its urgent priority. This is the case for the child-care package. It is only after such decisions that the ministry of health can also argue for an increased budget allocation at the expense of other ministries, using arguments preferably based on firm cause-and-effect relationships over time. If the arguments have to be based on assumptions rather than facts, this should be clearly stated. It is nothing to be ashamed of, because many other investments are also based on nothing other than assumptions. But any figures deriving from cost-effectiveness exercises are useful for, as Gish said of the budgeting process, 'anyone who can put up a number is likely to win'.

The integrated rural programme

It was agreed that MCH work and the components of MCH programmes are best dealt with under the broader heading of rural services. The difficulty came in the quantification of the components in the optimum package programme. One reason was the obvious overlap of costing; another was the lack of knowledge by medical practitioners of governments' budgeting techniques. Ministries in fact allocate against facilities and there are traditional ministerial divisions that allow for a calculation for rural and urban services as such. This needs to be made more explicit; the marking of each allocation to indicate whether it is to go to the urban area or to the rural areas has an extremely high priority.

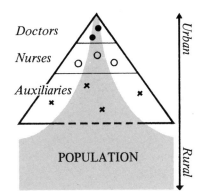

'Western' medicine:
the pyramid of elitism

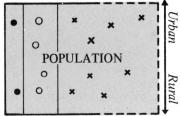

The broad front:
medicine by all, for all

**The way it is
and the way it could be**

The experience of many of the participants at the Addis Ababa seminar was that even if the ministry of health were given the money asked for, e.g. for the optimum package programme, it would probably not be able to spend it. It is repeatedly the case in many African countries that money for vaccines, for nutrition programmes and so on is not being spent. The fact is that most health inputs are outside the scope of the ministry of health; very often they are not provided by governments at all and thus have to be provided by the people themselves. There is a case for establishing two parallel ministries, with a ministry of health to correspond to the 'ministry of disease' (or medical ministry), with the latter subordinate to the former. This might permit the budgetary realignment that is necessary, reserving a more modest if no less significant role to traditional medicine, that of training specialist and non-specialist personnel, of monitoring medical aspects of rural health programmes and of planning for an amplified role for specialist medicine if and when economic circumstances make this possible. The task of the medical expert would then be similar to that carried out by, say, architects in relation to builders, one of design and consultation but not of implementation.

The delivery of health services is essentially a manpower question. Manpower costs generally take half of the recurrent budget of the ministry of health; this is true not only of Africa but virtually all round the world. Of that money over half goes to health workers, who at present may be classified in several ways. The horizontal division groups people in traditional areas, e.g. medical practitioners, nurses, laboratory technicians. In the vertical classification, doctors and specialists are at the top, a middle level has equivalents to technicians and, at the lowest level, there are the auxiliaries. Only those at the top of this ladder-like structure are called 'professionals'.

In this model, the fact that a village midwife may spend her working life in health service, perhaps supplying the only health help available, does not qualify her for consideration as a professional. There is a case for doing away with present nomenclature and calling everyone 'doctor' who has a formal health role. This would be a positive step towards the more democratic, more truly professional structuring that will be necessary if the narrow concept of disease treatment is to be replaced by the broader concept of health. It would certainly be better to substitute the word 'specialist' for that of 'professional' in the less-developed countries, since this would better reflect the realities. The fully trained physician is so rare there that he is, in any case, much more nearly equivalent to the 'specialist' of the developed country, who is only seen by referral.

Ratios for doctors but not for auxiliaries

The decisions about the staff mix for health programmes and the feasible/desirable ratios of medical personnel to population must be related to the cost of training and of employment. The erroneous assumption in doctor-to-population ratios is that doctors are the only health agents worthy of such statistical consideration.

Obviously it would be desirable to achieve a doctor-to-population ratio of 1:10,000 - yet this figure has been highly detrimental, particularly in Africa. For one thing, no doctor or any other health worker works in relation to population but rather in relation to facilities, interpreted very broadly, and such facilities are generally not available in rural areas. It is significant that, for auxiliaries, as has been pointed out, there are no targets, no objectives and no evaluation.

More auxiliaries, not more doctors

The participants all shared the view that health services in general and MCH services in particular in a less-developed country should be labour-intensive. Clearly, no formula is valid for all countries, whose circumstances differ. In a relatively advanced African country like Ghana (as far as MCH services are concerned) the mix would be markedly different from that of poorer African countries. But it is clear that a large cadre of auxiliaries is called for and this should be built on the basis of the principle of national coverage. This would represent a more realistic approach to comprehensiveness than that embodied in the present profession-oriented health services, which are sometimes national in name alone. Further coverage should be given by the use of unpaid village helpers and by cooperation with indigenous health workers (it should be possible to absorb, as the Chinese have done, the practitioners of traditional folk medicine within the local programme).

Transport

An important cost factor in the African context is that of transport. Mobile health teams have often been advocated, on grounds of flexibility and for other reasons. Moreover, some tactical health measures, such as immunization campaigns, may always be dependent upon the mobile team for their implementation. However, it needs to be recognized that, at present, adequate transport is not available to maintain a comprehensive centre-to-periphery service. Some steps are possible to improve the situation. In the first place, the integrated approach, particularly where expensive petrol-based road transport is concerned, requires that African governments should think carefully about maximizing the utility of all transport using the road network. Military trucks, commercial vans, public transport buses and private vehicles may all be making regular journeys to the same destination. There might be a case, therefore, for a centrally controlled road-transport authority that would be responsible for coordinating the various movements in order to avoid duplication of systems and the under-utilization of existing delivery journeys. There is also a case for developing a cheap, intermediate-technology vehicle (perhaps along the lines of the vehicle proposed by Ivan Illich), designed for African conditions and sponsored by a consortium of African countries.

The counterpart of this centre-based approach is a greater emphasis on the local service rather than on the 'mobile' concept. The weakness of the latter is that after the team has departed, the local situation reverts to what it was before, with a final result that is not long-lasting but impressionist and uneven. The promotion of the permanent local health service - no matter how rough-and-ready it might be in practice - would go a long way to resolving the communication problem, where transport is concerned, by creating a more enduring pressure to be brought to bear

upon making the best use of existing local transport for implementation, and by thinking in terms of getting the sick child to the clinic as well as in getting the team to the child.

Local orientation

The need is for an integrated approach and the health package will therefore constitute only one element within the rural service programme. In this context, there is a case for training workers in a variety of skills, on grounds of economy in both cost and labour. The medical bias, too, would be less dominating if the polyvalent worker were trained in an integrated framework rather than as a poor relation of doctors, within the hospital context. It is of considerable importance that such workers are recruited for training and service in their own local areas, for the worker who is removed for training to major urban centres may be reluctant to return to work in the countryside, once having been accustomed to the different cultural milieu of the city. The city offers many corrupting attractions and alternatives: political activities, alternative employment and contact with the urban unemployed, with the hope if not the real prospect of escape from rural hardship.

The drift to the towns increases the urban/rural gap and makes it even more difficult for the individual to take a direct part in the shaping of the environment. If the level of rural service is to be raised, the initiative and motivation must be generated at the grass roots and this will be greatly assisted by the creation of local cadres and the fostering of pride in the results of self-reliant activity. In this way, too, it will be easier to plan programmes in terms of real local needs, with the child as first priority, rather than in terms of abstract targets decided in the offices of ministries or international agencies.

We know, for instance, that the first step in some instances may have to be land reform, since community-based health services will remain phantoms as long as the real wealth of the rural areas is concentrated in the hands of a few individuals rather

The transport problem

than the mass of the people. In any event, there may be a case for decentralizing the ministry of health and for its substitution by a number of regional offices, in order to shift the emphasis away from the capital.

The field worker as an agent of change

Front-line health personnel should be looked upon as agents of change (Flahault, 1973). They establish a dialogue with the community that leads to a better-informed public. The demands are substantial and it is understandable, as Flahault points out, that front-line personnel, forced to perform miracles of ingenuity to compensate for the puny resources provided, sometimes are shocked or driven to despair by the ill-use of means available. It is therefore important to provide the local MCH personnel with back-up support in guidance and training with identification of the child as the primary problem. Staffing is not simply a question of numbers, control of quality is also necessary. This is an important point. It is desirable to promote self-reliance and attitudes of mind that are no longer based upon servility and the passive execution of orders transmitted 'down the ladder'. Local staff must be encouraged to take the initiative in a positive attack on local problems and delegation of responsibility is therefore essential. However, it must be borne in mind that local personnel will still be heavily dependent upon skilled expertise for information, guidance, instruction, the correction of mistakes and, if necessary, the redirection of their efforts. This should preferably be carried out in a spirit of friendly collaboration rather than of old-fashioned coercive direction. Local party leaders might well have a useful role to play here. The integrated cooperative training programme described by Monekosso in the first part of this book is of great interest and would merit further study and evaluation. Training has to be practical; it has to be undertaken near the area of future work; and it should be geared explicitly to actual function.

Leading from the front

Within this perspective, the role of the leader of the team is clear. It should be more that of a player-captain - first among equals - rather than that of the sole repository

Family welfare may include family planning

of authority whose pronouncements are awaited before decisions can be made. Much sophisticated writing has been devoted to 'scientific management methods' that are based on getting other people to do things. It should be said straight away that motivating local people themselves to introduce change is as important as the imposition of programme priorities from outside. This motivation can only be created by allowing people to follow up their own initiatives and thus to have some pride in their own achievements. It is known, too, that local needs - as these are revealed through local initiatives - often differ markedly from those identified at first sight by the outsider. The satisfaction of such needs is a motor for change.

The pilot project

The question of pilot projects was considered. There are known advantages in running pilot projects. The chief difficulty is that of replication. It is a common error by the outsider to think of African countries as broadly similar; actually, the socio-cultural, climatic and geographic differences within Africa may be in some ways greater than they are in other continents. It cannot be supposed, therefore, that there is some model that is valid for the whole of the continent. It was felt, none the less, that sufficient knowledge already existed to enable a programme to go ahead. Useful study projects are longitudinal, entail great delays and frequently give inconclusive results. If there is need for a pilot project, it would be as a 'lever' scheme: to dramatize the situation, to help convince the people in the country concerned that the solution lay in their hands and not in those of outsiders, and to provide the sparking-plug for more widespread adoption of the package programme. As such, the target of the project would not be to produce 'pure' research results but to see the integrated-approach child-care package actually functioning - and functioning well.

Conclusion

The Way Forward

Many of the participants at the Addis Ababa seminar believed that there was already sufficient knowledge in most of the fields discussed to justify going ahead with the optimum package programme. This is contrary to the view of an expert such as Taylor (1974), who believes that a logical service package that can be immediately implemented in a demonstration project cannot be developed by experts in joint discussion but needs to be evolved through 'intensive field research' in a small unit, so that it can be tested for replicability on a larger scale before general implementation. It is not easy to demonstrate that action programmes would lead to immediate success. For one thing, the results of such programmes are under-reported. A compilation of some 500 papers on the integration of family planning into MCH services, for example (DEIDS, 1973), revealed a striking lack of evaluation studies and concluded that most of the material continues to point out what should be done rather than to describe what has been done.

Perfect data for action will never be available

Further detailed knowledge is not essential for action, however, and there are grounds for concluding that the degree of perfection in research studies that is called for by western scholars reflects a reluctance to support the action that will itself - to the extent that it is successful - remove much of the need for further analysis. It may be that academically rigorous proof of viability will only ever be yielded by retrospective analysis of campaigns that have proved to be successful. If we are to wait for firm results and conclusions before acting, then we shall have to wait for a long time (longer than the life of the average government, for example, that may have authorized a study).

We have already observed the lack of reliable data of every kind that are needed in planning for children - data on number, age distribution, mortality, incidence of disease, on health, nutritional and educational status and cost, and on the utilization of health service coverage, for example - a lack so pronounced as to be worth classifying as a function of health-system failure in itself. The community health picture in the less-developed country is not known, except in broad outline, and for working purposes data are still used from industrialized countries of decades ago or from records of hospitals and clinics. There is also lack of knowledge about how and why children are affected by adverse early life experience and the role of implements in promoting cognitive development, and there is disagreement over the degree to which early stimulation is productive of enduring benefits; some evidence suggests that any improvement in primary-school performance from kindergarten experience may rapidly disappear (e.g. Reddy, 1971). Moreover, the detrimental effects of unfavourable environment during the early years (see Vahlquist and Yoloye above) may be less permanent since the genetic programmes underlying many cognitive and personality characteristics have not at that stage unfolded. There is evidence too of the later reversibility of the effects of social deprivation and also of severe malnutrition and it may be that the elements essential for normal growth and development are critical only in conjunction with or in the absence of other variables.

Health and nutrition education have produced disappointing results. It does not seem very easy to change people's food habits for the better in a poverty-stricken environment and food habits have in some ways worsened, notably in the substitution of less-valuable western products or technology for what were perfectly adequate before. Latham (1965) reported an estimate of production of 36.5 million gallons of human milk per annum for Tanzania; the cost of the same quantity in cow's milk for bottle-feeding would then have amounted to £9 million (say US$ 22.5 million). Studies of food habits and food availability have been elaborate and over-ambitious and the findings, often produced only after long delays are of questionable utility in changed social circumstances. Yet some experts consider that everything should be ready before the start of any programme and this implies exhausting all study approaches and possibilities before beginning. If the results in nutrition have so far been disappointing, it is probably because the attempts to produce food substitutes in programmatic form have been too complicated: actually during the weaning period, one extra meal a day from commonplace ingredients would give results equal in effectiveness to those of more sophisticated weaning foods.

A 'free' market means someone is still free to exploit the people

Some of the qualifications and objections to the local-delivery optimum package conceal a number of hidden interests and disingenuous attitudes. It is as well to recognize what these are. Political value systems still colour the thinking of those who recoil from the idea of training local health workers to full responsibility. In western medicine this finds a reflection in the refusal to allow 'access', in which entrenched privilege groups cultivate the myth of medical exclusiveness in order to guard their profits from the consumer in the market economy and fight hard to prevent the democratization of medicine (some dental work, for example, that could be carried out by prosthetic technicians is still reserved to 'dental surgeons'). These attitudes are projected on to the less-developed countries but it should be recognized that the values of the market economy are not of much use down at the exploited end of that value scale. The point of the package programme conceived as an integrated approach is that it should be planned with all structural imbalances taken into consideration. This need not have any direct political implications; the link between health service and political structure is not so intimate that the health services cannot change separately and independently within most socio-political systems, as the World Health Organization (1973) has pointed out.

Planning must begin with the fact of poverty

The fact remains that current dilemmas in development policy have their roots largely in the interrelationships between poverty and other 'failures' in the economic and social situation. It will do no good to pretend that solutions to the problem of child care in low-income countries lie elsewhere than in the framework of a realistic awareness of the nature of the political, social and economic milieu, in which the most difficult political breakthrough is in gaining acceptance of the need for total coverage. There may be no great improvement in the delivery of child-care services in the foreseeable future given present structures, since there may well be no great change in the present distribution of resources either within or outside the health sector. In the poorest of African countries, therefore, there will not be the funds for 'intensive field research' in even a small unit, and less chance of such an initiative achieving general implementation. Research-oriented schemes are likely to add themselves to other failures in Africa, which has been called the graveyard of education experiments. If the project is not run by local people, experience shows that it will fade away when the expatriate goes back to enjoy his higher standard of living in his home country. There is need for a project, but not for a project with only research justification: it should be a project that would illustrate its own values in action rather than a dry run for some further scheme in a yet-more-delayed future.

The integrated approach

Kisa reminded the seminar that the services which children require need an integrated approach if they are to have the most effective impact on child development. Not all services that are essential for the proper development of the child are the responsibility of the ministry of health and, since other ministries are involved and other agencies outside the government, there is a need to coordinate the planning of services for children. Most ministries are organized on a vertical line of communication, but what is required is horizontal coordination if a programme for children is to be successful. The seminar itself demonstrated the possibilities for the integrated approach in terms of interdisciplinary collaboration.

The need for an integrated system in the health sector (as elsewhere) becomes clear upon examination of a typical breakdown of national health inputs, with its evident duplication and lack of coordination of effort: (1) ministry of health budget (whole population), *one-third*; (2) WHO campaigns (selective by disease, etc.), *one-third*; (3) missionary work (independent and uncoordinated with the other inputs), *one-fifth*; (4) armed forces (duplication), *up to one-fifth*; (5) private sector (may not include brain-drain cost), say, *one-twentieth.* It should be noted how small a part of the total budget even for disease elimination is under the control of the ministry of health. This pattern could be repeated for transport and the servicing of industrial and commercial outlets, with many parallel and wasteful systems operating simultaneously. It cannot be stressed too strongly that poor communications and inadequate transport networks present such a serious problem that, from the standpoint of general health - as with the lack of demographic and other data for planning - their inadequacy must also be rated as a medical problem. The design of the package must therefore in some way write in the transport dimension, which will vary in gravity by region or community.

A further parameter of vital importance is water: this presents as important a focus of concern at the local level as does the need for valid planning data at the ministerial level. As Bradley (1970) pointed out, we do not know what the consequences are of partial or isolated improvement of water supplies and what rate of improvement is possible. (The need for caution in the handling of water has to be noted, of course, in view of the fact that some water-development schemes may increase the spread of parasite diseases.) But the link between economic considerations and the level of public health can be seen in water management. Irrigation schemes, copious supply of uncontaminated water, domestic and public hygiene based on water and sanitation - these are correlated with development and the improvement of public health. They are evidently beneficial even though it is difficult to demonstrate the exact cause-and-effect relationships that are at work. Olivier (1974) has also described, for parasitology, the way in which existing evidence fails to provide answers to the most important questions put by health planners, but notes that the economic effect is two-way ('economic factors influence the prevalence and severity of parasitic infections'). The parasitic diseases

offer a special economic challenge to the developing world and 'parasitologists should learn at least the essentials of medical economics and understand something of the methods, tools and attitudes of economists'.

Delivery through the local health workers and local centre

The method of delivery of the health programme must also be built into the integrated package, if it is not to remain an abstraction. This must be, substantially, by means of the local health worker, operating through the local centre. In a full national system this would entail the remodelling of the health structure, since the redistribution of resources that village-oriented health care implies would lead to the break-up of the present elitist structure. Probably the urban ministry of health would be virtually dismantled, as it was in China, and all trained staff would be directed to the countryside for a period of ten years or more to help establish the local medical centres. No large hospitals would be built during this period but the budget allocation for them would be used for health-delivery units of the smallest size for the support to the village health worker and for the administrative and human effectiveness of these units. In practice such a general transformation may not be immediately very likely in most of Africa, since it depends for its success on a degree of popular consensus and collective awareness that are still a long way off. The essence of the package, however, should be its viability in the achievement of intermediate goals: in this light a full national system is not the first essential, provided the package is able to meet the need to be maximally polyvalent and integrative at its own level of delivery in the rural context. There is no political target as such - unless the good health of all children is to be thought of as a politically motivated aim - and the package approach is therefore acceptable within any ideology and also generally attractive in that it holds out hope of better return on investment. The problem for the medical profession is to define exactly the signs and symptoms to which the local health worker has to react and to outline the steps to be taken in each situation. The training of supportive health staff in specific rural health technology must have high priority and a new role has to be developed for the hospital. What is sure is that local health workers are necessary for

Women bringing water. The Package may be sinking a well. . .

implementation: without their active participation and control no field project will survive.

What are we waiting for?

The failure of communication

It may be that we wait because of a failure in another element that we have not so far discussed: communication. The least that can be said for the optimum package concept is that it will have a cumulative effect, that it will provide cost-effective answers and that it will help to engage the energies of the mass of the people via the initial involvement of the local health worker. But there is more to it than that, in the failure of communication not to have succeeded in illustrating the further possibilities. There may be a case for a nation-wide review of the means of communication, in the context of integrated programmes, with a view to exerting greater control over the direction of public thinking. The fact is that the rural health-care programme will only succeed at all if the need for it, and its urgency, are communicated - to those in authority in government in Africa, to those medical practitioners and planners who are prepared to look a little further afield than their immediate preoccupations and to officials in the United Nations system not only in the health agencies and Unicef but also in the economic and social organs looking for cost-effective or cost-effectiveness projects to support. It was felt at the seminar that the gulf between the disciplines involved in planning and implementing child-care programmes was negligible compared with the gulf that had to be spanned to reach some educated lay people and the politicians. The public at large needs to be informed, for there is confusion about both ends and means. There is a greater scepticism about the value of aid, thought of as false charity, in view of the continued economic plundering of the third-world countries by the rich - but there is a corresponding willingness to cooperate with projects that hold out the hope of reaching intermediate goals. It is hoped that this book will itself help to broaden the communication flow. If it is true that much published material is hortatory rather rather than descriptive, this may be attributed in part to the need to generate sufficient motivation for progress.

The package must 'design itself' according to local needs

Progress in evaluating costs can best be made by studying the total effects of the package in an on-going situation. Facts on costs are a valuable first step. There should be a breakdown of costs for various types of diseases and for unit expenditures. The design of each component of the package can be substantially improved by cost-effectiveness studies as modelled earlier in this book. There is need for some effort to establish what the minimum nutritional margins are, in the rural African setting, based not on arbitrary standards (witness the case of the disastrous doctor ratios), but on the African context itself, varied as that is with its wealth of languages and peoples. The integrated child-care package would therefore be tailored, by degrees, as an operational project until it was optimal for the child health of a particular community, concentrating its fire on those among all the unfavourable factors that are predominant at each stage of the community's development, with the village participating in setting its own priorities. It is hoped that at some stage during progress in the development of the package, a level will be reached at which birth control will be sought after. Help for infertile couples may also be made available then.

Helping the children will also help to build a better society for tomorrow

The sheer size of the childhood population, the child's vulnerability during the toddler stage and the possibility of preventing death through better use of existing statistical and financial resources make expenditure on children the most important of human investments. Those children who grow up in a life-enhancing environment will become adults who are more self-aware and conscious of their situation and problems and confident that it is possible to act on the environment, to mould it rather than to be moulded. In poor countries the best way for the health worker to reach the rural pre-school child (where there are few schools or MCH centres) may well be through education of (and help to) women, especially mothers. This is another communication problem, in part; something actually happening on the spot, even if it is not the best possible subprogramme, has a fundamental value in generating pressures and activity from below. That 'something happening on the spot' could well be streamlined curative medicine, which often has dramatic results. This is the value of the Chinese example, both as a general model for what is possible for a country starting from the bottom and also in the approach and help for women. It will be possible to make better judgements on the merits or the effectiveness of the Chinese system when more objective data are available, but it is already clear that much can be done when the energies of the mass of the population are mobilized to achieve such targets. The problem in Africa is that the resources are simply not available to underwrite the sort of services that are now commonplace in China.

The need for a special initiative to help the children

An important virtue of economic analysis for medical programmes lies in its utility for discussion when arguments are needed to persuade planning and finance ministries, or international agencies, to back investment in human resources as well as in economic growth objectives. UNDP and other financing agencies need to know of the economic justification for health programmes if they are to evaluate priorities where social and human considerations are concerned. The problem of child health has been obscured for too long by being subsumed within the general targets of UN and other programmes. There is need for a new initiative for a permanent programme that would be specifically charged with the survival needs of children. The executing body would have the special responsibility of directing the rural optimum-package programme in collaboration with interested governments. The role of the multilateral or bilateral aid in this case would be limited to technological infrastructure: the package would be delivered by the local health worker and the multilateral (or bilateral) assistance would not go beyond the analysis of data and liaison with higher authority. There might in this setting be need for a polyvalent worker on the support side (as a counterpart to the polyvalent health worker), who would combine some economic, managerial and statistical expertise with general health skills. The child-care package although distinct, would need to be integrated into the rural development programme as a whole.

Bibliography

The list of general references is intended to provide an overview of works of general interest in this field, not all of which are necessarily cited in the text.

General references

Akhtar, S. 1975. *Health Care in the People's Republic of China. A Bibliography with Abstracts.* Ottawa, International Development Research Centre. (IDRC-0380.)

Bryant, J. 1969. *Health and the Developing World.* New York, N.Y., Cornell University Press.

Cochrane, A.L. 1972. *Effectiveness and Efficiency: Random Reflections on Health Services.* London, Nuffield Provincial Hospitals Trust.

Dag Hammarskjöld Foundation, The. 1975. *The 1975 Dag Hammarskjöld Report on Development and International Cooperation.* Uppsala, the Foundation. *(Development Dialogue,* 1975, No. 1/2.) (Also published in French and Spanish.)

Elliott, K.; Knight, J. (eds.). 1974. *Human Rights in Health.* Elsevier, Excerpta Medica, North Holland. (Ciba Foundation Symp. 23, new ser.)

Ewans, J.L. 1970. *Children in Africa. A Review of Psychological Research.* New York, N.Y., Teachers' College Press, Teachers' College, Columbia University.

Fuglesang, A. 1973. *Applied Communication in Developing Countries: Ideas and Observations.* Uppsala, Dag Hammarskjöld Foundation.

Grundy, F.; Reinke, W.A. 1973. *Health Practice Research and Formalized Managerial Methods.* Geneva, WHO. (Publ. Hlth Pap., No. 51.)

Hilleboe, H.E.; Barkhuus, A.; Thomas, Jr., W.C. 1972. *Approaches to National Health Planning.* Geneva, WHO. (Publ. Hlth Pap. No. 46.)

Hoorweg, J. 1972. Africa (South of the Sahara). Review of Psychological Literature. In: V.S. Sexton and H. Misiak (eds.), *Psychology Around the World Today.* Monterey, Calif., Brooks/Cole, 1973. (Mimeo.: Leyden, Neth., Africa Study Centre, 1972.)

King, M.; King, F.; Morley, D.; Burgess, L.; Burgess, A. 1972. *Nutrition for Developing Countries.* Nairobi, Oxford University Press.

Morley, D. 1973. *Paediatric Priorities in the Developing World.* Butterworths, London.

Puffer, R.R.; Serrano, C.V. 1973. *Patterns of Mortality in Childhood.* Pan American Health Organization/WHO.

Roemer, M.I. 1972. *Evaluation of Community Health Centers.* Geneva, WHO. (Publ. Hlth Pap. No. 48.)

United Nations Children's Fund (Unicef)/ United Nations Economic and Social Council (Ecosoc). March 1974. *The Young Child: Approaches to Action in Developing Countries.*

Vahlquist, B. (ed.). 1972. *Nutrition. A Priority in African Development.* Uppsala, Dag Hammarskjöld Foundation.

White, G.F.; Bradley, D.J.; White, A.U. 1972. *Drawers of Water: Domestic Water Use in East Africa.* Chicago & London, University of Chicago Press.

World Health Organization (WHO)/Unicef. February 1975. *Joint Study on Alternative Approaches to Meeting Basic Health Needs of Populations in Developing Countries.* WHO/ Unicef Joint Committee on Health Policy.

Special references

Addis Ababa. Central Statistical Office and Municipality of. Population of Addis Ababa. *Stat. Bull.,* No.8.

American Public Health Association. 1972. *Development and evaluation of integrated delivery systems (DEIDS).*

Arole, R.; Arole, M. 1975. *Health by the People.* Geneva, WHO.

Aykroyd, W.R.; Kevany, J.P. 1973. Mortality in Infancy and Early Childhood in Ireland, Scotland, England and Wales, 1871 to 1971. *Ecol.Food Nutr.,* 2: 11.

Azurin, J.C.; Alvero, M. 1971. Cholera Incidence in Population Offered Cholera Vaccination: Comparison of Cooperative and Uncooperative Groups. *Bull.Wld Hlth Org.,* 44: 815.

Bengoa, J.M. 1970. Recent Trends in the Public Health Aspects of Protein-calorie Malnutrition. *WHO Chron.,* 24: 552.

Bradley, D.J. 1970. Health Problems of Water Management. *J.Trop.Med.,* 73: 286.

—. 1974. Water Supplies: the Consequences of Change. In: *Human Rights in Health.* Amsterdam, Elsevier. (Ciba Foundation Symp. 23.)

Bryant, J.; Jenkins, D. 1971. *Moral Issues and Health Care.* Geneva, Christian Medical Commission, World Council of Churches. *(Contact,* Occ. Pap. No.4.)

—. *Health Care, Human Values and Decision Making.* 1973. (Mimeo.)

CENDES. 1965. *Health Planning. Problems of Concept and Method.* (Pan-American Health Organization.)

Clarke, A.D.B. 1972. Consistency and Variability in the Growth of Human Characteristics. *Dev.Med.Child Neurol.,* 14: 668.

Cvjetanović, B. 1973. Immunization Programmes. *WHO Chron.,* 27: 66.

Flahault, D. 1973. The Training of Front Line Health Personnel in Development. *WHO Chron.,* 27: 236.

Freij, L.; Sterky, G.; Gebeyehu, T. 1973. The Components and Economics of a Small Scale Urban Mother and Child Health Clinic. *Ethiop.Med.J.,* 11: 101.

Grab, B.; Cvjetanović, B. 1971. Simple Method for Rough Determination of the Cost-Benefit Balance Point of Immunization Programmes. *Bull.Wld Hlth Org.,* 45: 536.

Hutchison, G.B. 1960. Evaluation of Preventive Services. *J.Chron.Dis.,* 5: 497.

Jelliffe, D.B.; Jelliffe, E.F.P. (eds.). 1972. Nutrition Programs for Pre-school Children. Zagreb Guidelines. *Am. J.Clin.Nutr.,* 25: 595.

John, T.J.; Jayabal, P.K. 1972. Oral Polio Vaccination of Children in the Tropics. I: The Poor Sero-Conversion Rates and the Absence of Viral Interference. *Am.J.Epidemiol.,* 96: 263

Kidane, Y.; Freij, L.; Sterky, G.; Wall, S. January 1975 *Determinants of Child Health. A Case Study in Addis Ababa.* Addis Ababa, Ethiopian Nutrition Institute. (Mimeo.)

Kingma, S.J. February 1975. Primary Health Care and the Village Health Worker. *Contact* (Geneva), No. 25. (Christian Medical Commission, World Council of Churches.)

Klarman, H.E. 1965. *The Economics of Health.* New York, N.Y., Columbia University Press.

—. Spring 1974. Application of Cost Benefit Analysis to the Health Services and the Special Case of Technologic Innovation. *Int.J. Hlth Serv.*, 4: 325.

Levin, A.L. 1968. Cost Effectiveness in Maternal and Child Health. Implications for Program Planning and Evaluation. *New Engl.J.Med.*, 278: 1041.

Liang, M.H.; Eichling, P.S.; Fine, L.J.; Annas, G.J. 1973. Chinese Health Care: Determinants of the System. *Am.J. Publ.Hlth*, Vol. 63, No. 102.

Lindholm, B. 1973. (Benefits and Costs of Poliomyelitis Vaccination.) *Läkartidningen*, 70: 1174. (In Swedish.)

Long, E.C. 1972. Problems in Delivering Health Care in Central America. *Trop.Doct.*, 2: 89.

McKay, H.; McKay, A.; Sinisterra, L. 1973. *Stimulation of Intellectual and Social Competence in Colombian Preschool Age Children Affected by the Multiple Deprivation of Depressed Urban Environments (Second Progress Report).* Cali, Human Ecology Research Station.

Minkowski, A. 1973. Health of Mother and Child: The Experience in the People's Republic of China, the Democratic Republic of Viet-Nam, and Cuba. *Impact Sci. Soc.*, 23: 29.

Molnos, A. 1972. *Cultural Source Materials for Population Planning in East Africa,* Vol. I -III. Nairobi, East African Publishing House.

Mönckeberg, F.B. 1973. Infant Feeding and Weaning Practice: the Problem as It Exists in Developing Countries. *Austral.Ped. J.Suppl.*, 2: 48.

Olivier, L.J. 1974. The Economics of Human Parasitic Infections. *Z. Parasitenk.*, 45: 197.

Rasmusson, R. 1972. Kenyan Rural Development and Aid. A Case Study on Effects of Assistance on Planning and Implementation for the Special Rural Development Programme, and Proposals for Improvement. *Dev.Stud.*, No. 2.

Read, M. 1966. *Culture, Health and Disease.* London, Tavistock/Lippincott.

Reddy, P.H. 1971. Preparing the Child for Primary School. *Carn.Enf.,* 16: 45.

Rifkin, S.B. 1973. Health Care in China: Put Prevention First. *Carn.Enf.,* Vol.23, No.35.

Rifkin, C.B. December 1972. China and the Less Developed Nations. *Contact* (Geneva), No.12. (Christian Medical Commission, World Council of Churches.)

Savosnick, K.M. 1972. An Economist's View of Nutrition in its Struggle for Budgetary Priority. In: Bo Vahlquist (ed.), *Nutrition, A Priority in African Development.* Uppsala, The Dag Hammarskjöld Foundation.

Scrimshaw, N.S. 1974. Myths and Realities in International Health Planning. *Am.J.Publ.Hlth,* 64: 792.

Seccombe, E.W.C. 1970. The Appraisal of Health Service Projects Using Cost-Benefit Analysis. *Wld Hosp.,* 6: 214.

Seers, D. 1969. *The Meaning of Development.* Brighton, Institute of Development Studies. (Communication ser.No. 44.)

—. 1972. *The Prevalence of Pseudo-planning.*

Singer, H. 1972. *Children in the Strategy of Development.* New York, N.Y., United Nations Centre for Economic and Social Information.

Spence, J.; Walton, W.S.; Miller, F.J.W.; Court, S.D.M. 1954. *A Thousand Families in Newcastle upon Tyne.* London, Oxford University Press.

Tafari, N.; Ross, M. 1973. On the Need for Organized Perinatal Care. *Eth.Med.J.,* 11: 93.

Tafesse, B. 1973. Analysis of Admissions to the Ethio-Swedish Paediatric Clinic. *Ethiop.Med.J.,* 11:1.

Tayback, M.; Prince, J.S. 1965. Infant Mortality and Fertility in Five Towns of Ethiopia. *Ethiop.Med.J.,* 4: 11.

Taylor, E.C. 1974. Challenge to the Agencies - A New Era in International Health. *Focus: Technical Cooperation,* No.3. (Quarterly supplement to *Int.Dev.Rev.,* Vol.XVI, No.3.)

United Nations Children's Fund. 1973. *Children and Adolescents in the Second Development Decade. Priorities for Planning and Action.* Unicef. (E/JCEF/627.)

Waaler, H.T.; Piot, M.A. 1969. The Use of an Epidemiological Model for Estimating the Effectiveness of Tuberculosis Control Measures. *Bull.Wld Hlth Org.,* Vol.41.

Warren, N. 1972. African Infant Precocity. *Psychol. Bull.,* 78, No.5: 353-67.

White, G.F.; Bradley, D.J.; White, A.U. 1972. *Drawers of Water: Domestic Water Use in East Africa.* Chicago & London, University of Chicago Press.

Woodruff, A.W. (Chairman). 1975. Measles Vaccination in Developing Countries. A Symposium on Current Issues. *Roy. Soc.Trop.Med.Hyg.,* 69: 21-34.

World Health Organization (WHO). 1972. *The Prevention of Perinatal Morbidity and Mortality.* Geneva, the Organization. (Publ.Hlth Pap., No.42.)

—. 1970. *The Prevention of Perinatal Morbidity and Mortality.* Geneva, the Organization. (Tech.Rep.Ser., No. 457.)

—. January 1973. *Organizational Study on Methods of Promoting the Development of Basic Health Services.*

Lists of Participants, Resource Persons, Observers and Organizers

Participants

Beatrice B.A. Asirifi   *Social welfare worker*
Principal, National Day Care Training Centre, Department
of Social Welfare and Community Development, P.O. Box
M230, Accra (Ghana)

Phoebe Asiyo   *Social welfare worker*
Executive Officer, Child Welfare Society of Kenya, P.O.
Box 43982, Nairobi (Kenya)

Assefa Mehretu   *Development researcher*
Director, Institute of Development Research, Haile
Sellassie I University, P.O. Box 1176, Addis Ababa
(Ethiopia)

E. Maweje Bakoja   *Public health administrator*
Principal Medical Officer in charge of MCH and Health
Education, Ministry of Health, P.O. Box 8, Entebbe
(Uganda)

Aaron D. Chiduo   *Public health administrator*
Director of Curative Services, Ministry of Health, P.O. Box
9083, Dar es Salaam (Tanzania)

Monica Fisher   *Public health administrator*
School Medical Officer, Ministry of Health, P.O. Box 2691,
Kitwe (Zambia)

Rabi Iliasu   *Public health administrator*
Principal Nursing Officer, Ministry of Health and Social
Welfare, Kano State, Kano (Nigeria)

Salvator Kanani   *Public health administrator*
Assistant Director of Medical Services, Ministry of Health,
P.O. Box 30016, Nairobi (Kenya)

Valerian P. Kimati   *Paediatrician*
Senior Medical Officer in Paediatrics, Mwanza Hospital,
P.O. Box 1370, Mwanza (Tanzania)

Jack J. Kisa   *Development planner*
Principal Economist, Ministry of Finance and Planning,
P.O. Box 30007, Nairobi, Kenya
Present position:
Chief, JASPA, ILO Regional Office for Africa, P.O. Box
2788, Addis Ababa (Ethiopia)

Yuyi K. Libakeni   *Development planner*
Acting Deputy Director of Planning, Development Planning
Division, Ministry of Development Planning and National
Guidance, P.O. Box RW268, Lusaka (Zambia)

Adetokunbo O. Lucas *Public health specialist*
Professor of Preventive and Social Medicine, University of
Ibadan, Ibadan (Nigeria)

Bwembya Lukutati   *Social welfare planner*
Director of Social Welfare, Ministry of Labour and Social
Services, P.O. Box RW81, Lusaka (Zambia)

Maaza Bekele   *Development planner*
Head, Social Services Department, Planning Commission,
P.O. Box 1037, Addis Ababa, (Ethiopia)

Mehari Gebre-Medhin   *Nutrition administrator*
Deputy Director, Ethiopian Nutrition Institute, P.O. Box 5654, Addis Ababa, Ethiopia

Mesfin Demissie   *Public health administrator*
Provincial Medical Officer, Sidamo Province, P.O. Box 51, Awassa (Ethiopia)

Mechtildis Mufwaya   *Public health administrator*
Senior Public Health Nurse, Ministry of Health, P.O. Box 205, Lusaka (Zambia)

Dunstan J. Njau   *Rural development administrator*
Assistant Commissioner for Rural Development, Prime Minister's Office, P.O. Box 3021, Dar es Salaam (Tanzania)

Eric Odotei   *Development planner*
Economics Officer, Manpower Division, Ministry of Finance and Economic Planning, P.O. Box M76, Accra (Ghana)

Martin L. Oduori   *Paediatrician*
Senior Consultant Paediatrician, Kenyatta National Hospital, P.O. Box 30024, Nairobi (Kenya)

Samuel Ofosu-Amaah   *Paediatrician*
Senior Lecturer in Child Health, Department of Community Health, University of Ghana Medical School, P.O. Box 4236, Accra (Ghana)

Francis P. Okediji   *Sociologist*
Professor and Head, Department of Sociology, University of Ibadan, Ibadan (Nigeria)

S. Kegenge Ongeri   *Paediatrician*
Lecturer, Department of Paediatrics, Faculty of Medicine, University of Nairobi, P.O. Box 30588, Nairobi (Kenya)

Irene Thomas   *Public health administrator*
Principal Medical Officer in charge of MCH and Family Planning Programmes, Federal Ministry of Health, Yakubu Gowon Street, Lagos (Nigeria)

Yayehirad Kitaw   *Public health specialist*
Lecturer and Head, Department of Preventive Medicine and Public Health, Faculty of Medicine, Haile Sellassie University, P.O. Box 1176, Addis Ababa (Ethiopia)

Khalda Zahir   *Public health administrator*
Assistant Under-Secretary in charge of Maternal and Child Health, Ministry of Health, Khartoum (Sudan)

Resource persons

Fikre Workeneh   *Psychiatrist*
Assistant Professor, Department of Medicine, Faculty of Medicine, Haile Sellassie I University, P.O. Box 1176, Addis Ababa (Ethiopia)

Oscar Gish   *Health economist*
Adviser to the Ministry of Health, P.O. Box 9083, Dar es Salaam (Tanzania)
Present position:
Research Officer, Institute of Development Studies, University of Sussex, Brighton BN1 9RE (United Kingdom)

Derrick B. Jelliffe   *Public health specialist*
Professor and Head, Division of Population, Family and International Health, School of Public Health, University of California, Los Angeles, California 90024 (USA)

Ulla Larsson   *Paediatrician*
Head of Child Health Care, Department of Paediatrics, Linköping University, S-581 85 Linköping (Sweden)

Yngve Larsson   *Public health administrator*
Professor, Department of Paediatrics, Linköping University, S-581 85 Linköping (Sweden)

Lin Chuan-chia   *Paediatrician*
Head of Child Health Care Department, Peking Children's Hospital, Peking (People's Republic of China)

Li Pao-ai   *Paediatrician*
Head of the Paediatric Department, Teaching Hospital,
Tientsin Medical College, Tientsin (People's Republic of
China)

Ernst Michanek   *Development assistance administrator*
Chairman of the Board of Trustees, The Dag Hammarskjöld
Foundation, Director-General, Swedish International
Development Authority (SIDA), S-105 25 Stockholm
(Sweden)

G.L. Monekosso   *Public health specialist*
Professeur, Directeur du Centre Universitaire des Sciences de
la Santé, L'Université Fédérale du Caméroun, B.P. 1364,
Yaoundé (Cameroon)

T. Peter Omari   *Sociologist*
Chief, Social Development Section, United Nations
Economic Commission for Africa, P.O. Box 3005, Addis
Ababa (Ethiopia)

Otikoye Ransom-Kuti *Paediatrician*
Professor and Chairman, Department of Paediatrics,
College of Medicine, University of Lagos, P.M.B. 12003,
Lagos (Nigeria)

Teshome Wagaw   *Psychologist*
Associate Professor and Head, Department of Educational
Psychology, Haile Sellassie I University, P.O. Box 1176,
Addis Ababa (Ethiopia)

Bo Vahlquist   *Paediatrician*
Professor, Department of Paediatrics, Uppsala University
Hospital, S-750 14 Uppsala (Sweden)

Emmanuel A. Yoloye   *Educationist*
Professor of Education, University of Ibadan, Ibadan
(Nigeria)

Observers

Bo Akerren   *Public health administrator*
Director, Ethiopian Nutrition Institute, P.O. Box 5654,
Addis Ababa (Ethiopia)
Present position:
Adviser to the Ministry of Health, Kuala Lumpur (Malaysia)

Aklilu Habte   *Education administrator*
President, Haile Sellassie I University, P.O. Box 1176, Addis
Ababa (Ethiopia)
Present position:
Minister for Culture, Addis Ababa (Ethiopia)

Gunnar Arhammar   *Paediatrician*
MCH Adviser, Ministry of Health, P.O. Box 205, Lusaka
(Zambia)

A. Catipovic   *Public health planner*
Planning Division, Ministry of Public Health, P.O. Box 1234,
Addis Ababa (Ethiopia)

Greta Hedenström   *Paediatrician*
Dr Hålens gata 3, S-413 23 Gothenburg (Sweden)

E.F. Patrice Jelliffe   *Nutritionist*
School of Public Health, University of California, Los
Angeles, California 90024 (USA)

A.K. Joppa   *Child health planner*
Planning Officer, Unicef, P.O. Box 44145, Nairobi (Kenya)

Gunlög Lundgren   *Development assistance administrator*
Department of Public Health, Swedish International
Development Authority (SIDA), S-105 25 Stockholm
(Sweden)

Solomon Ayalew   *Public health planner*
Planning Division, Ministry of Public Health, P.O. Box 1234,
Addis Ababa (Ethiopia)

A.H. Thomas   *Public health administrator*
World Health Organization, Liaison Officer with the
Economic Commission for Africa, P.O. Box 3005, Addis
Ababa (Ethiopia)

Organizing committee
Göran Sterky (Chairman)   *Paediatrician*
Professor and Hospital Director, Ethio-Swedish Paediatric
Clinic, P.O. Box 1768, Addis Ababa (Ethiopia)
Present position:
Associate Professor of Paediatrics, Karolinska Institutet,
St Görans Hospital, Box 12500, S-112 81 Stockholm
(Sweden)
Demissie Habte   *Paediatrician*
Associate Professor of Paediatrics, Ethio-Swedish Paediatric
Clinic, P.O. Box 1768, Addis Ababa (Ethiopia)
Present position:
Head, Department of Paediatrics, National University,
Addis Ababa (Ethiopia)
Nebiat Tafari   *Paediatrician*
Assistant Professor of Paediatrics, Ethio-Swedish Paediatric
Clinic, P.O. Box 1768, Addis Ababa (Ethiopia)
Pietros Hadgu   *Paediatrician*
Assistant Professor of Paediatrics, Ethio-Swedish Paediatric
Clinic, P.O. Box 1768, Addis Ababa (Ethiopia)
Andreas Fuglesang   *Communication specialist*
Adviser, Ethiopian Nutrition Institute, P.O. B. 5654,
Addis Ababa (Ethiopia)
James Riby-Williams   *Social development planner*
Director, Human Resources Division, United Nations
Economic Commission for Africa, P.O. Box 3001, Addis
Ababa (Ethiopia)

Dag Hammarskjöld Foundation
Sven Hamrell
Executive Director, the Foundation, Övre Slottsgatan 2,
S-752 20 Uppsala (Sweden)
Olle Nordberg
Assistant Director, the Foundation, Övre Slottsgatan 2,
S-752 20 Uppsala (Sweden)
Peter Phillips
Production Editor, *Development Dialogue,* the Foundation,
Övre Slottsgatan 2, S-752 20 Uppsala (Sweden)

Secretariat
Pamela Stilling
Susanne Gebre Medhin
Habtinesh Gessesse
Joy Luscombe

Acknowledgements are due to the following for permission
to use copyright photographs: Nils-Erik Ekstrand (page 81);
FAO (cover, pages 63, 95, 187); Per Gunvall (page 181);
Bo-Erik Gyberg (pages 31, 77, 91, 197, 212, 224, 229); Jean
Hermansson (page 2); Stig Holmqvist (page 129); Per L-B
Nilsson (page 85); Bertil Odén (page 130); Esben H. Thorning
(page 191); UNECA (pages 59, 177); UNESCO (page 121);
WHO (page 215).